Praise for Simon Sebag Montefiore's

Written in History

"If you loved Ernst Gombrich's *A Little History of the World* and are in the mood for another . . . global history from a different angle, this collection of historically significant letters through the ages compiled by Simon Sebag Montefiore might well hit the spot. . . . He has distilled a few millennia of world history into 240 extremely un-boring pages. . . . Montefiore has an eye for the spicy, the horrifying, the passionate and the shocking. . . . Very moving." —*The Times* (London)

"Some [letters] are truly revolutionary and visionary. . . . Others are very personal. . . . But all are fascinating, as are the compiler's comments on each letter, little gems . . . in their own right." —*Daily Mail* (London)

"*Written in History* is a search through the millennia, the result an astonishing array: all human life is here encapsulated, in just a few paragraphs or even just a sentence; all are surprising, and mostly unfamiliar. . . . Everything here is a revelatory marvel, whether a hideous rant from the Marquis de Sade (1783), or the impassioned logic of religious tolerance from Babur to his son Humayun (1529). Truly the spectrum of human belief and behavior is revealed in this selection." —*The Arts Desk*

Simon Sebag Montefiore

Written in History

Simon Sebag Montefiore is a prizewinning historian whose bestselling books have been published in more than forty-eight languages. *Catherine the Great & Potemkin* was shortlisted for the Samuel Johnson Prize; *Stalin: The Court of the Red Tsar* won the History Book of the Year Prize at the British Book Awards; *Young Stalin* won the Costa Biography Award, Los Angeles Times Biography Prize, and Le Grand Prix de la Biographie Politique; *Jerusalem: The Biography* won the Jewish Book Council's Book of the Year Prize and the Wenjin Award from the National Library of China; *The Romanovs: 1613–1918* won the Lupicaia del Terriccio Book Prize. Montefiore is also the author of the acclaimed Moscow Trilogy of novels *Sashenka*, *Red Sky at Noon* and *One Night in Winter*, which won the Political Fiction of the Year Prize. He received his PhD in history at Cambridge University and now lives in London with his wife, the novelist Santa Montefiore, and their two children.

www.simonsebagmontefiore.com
@simonmontefiore

Written in History

Letters That Changed the World

Simon Sebag Montefiore

Vintage Books

A DIVISION OF PENGUIN RANDOM HOUSE LLC

NEW YORK

FIRST VINTAGE BOOKS EDITION, NOVEMBER 2019

Copyright © 2018 by Simon Sebag Montefiore

Originally published in hardcover in Great Britain by Weidenfeld &
Nicolson, an imprint of The Orion Publishing Group Ltd., London, in 2018.
Published by arrangement with The Orion Publishing Group Ltd.
First published in the United Kingdom in 2018. All rights reserved.
Published in the United States by Vintage Books, a division of
Penguin Random House LLC, New York.

Vintage and colophon are registered
trademarks of Penguin Random House LLC.

Pages 297–304 constitute an extension of this copyright page.

Library of Congress Cataloging-in-Publication Data
Names: Sebag Montefiore, Simon, 1965– editor.
Title: Written in history : letters that changed the world /
Simon Sebag Montefiore.
Description: First Vintage Books edition. | New York : Vintage Books,
a division of Penguin Random House LLC, 2019.
Identifiers: LCCN 2019028006 (print) | LCCN 2019028007 (ebook)
Subjects: LCSH: Letters.
Classification: LCC PN6131 .W77 2019 (print) | LCC PN6131 (ebook) |
DDC 808.86—dc23
LC record available at https://lccn.loc.gov/2019028006

**Vintage Trade Paperback ISBN: 978-1-9848-9816-6
eBook ISBN: 978-1-9848-9817-3**

*Author photograph © Sasha Sebag-Montefiore
Book design by Nick Alguire*

www.vintagebooks.com

Printed in the United States of America
10 9 8 7 6 5 4 3 2 1

To Lily Bathsheba

Contents

Introduction. xix

Love

Henry VIII to Anne Boleyn, May 1528 3

Frida Kahlo to Diego Rivera, undated 5

Thomas Jefferson to Maria Cosway,
12 October 1786 7

Catherine the Great to Prince Potemkin,
c.19 March 1774 11

James I to George Villiers, Duke of
Buckingham, 17 May 1620 13

Vita Sackville-West to Virginia Woolf,
21 January 1926 15

Between Suleiman the Magnificent
and Hurrem Sultan, c.1530s 17

Anaïs Nin to Henry Miller, c.August 1932 . . . 19

Alexandra to Rasputin, 1909 23

Horatio Nelson to Emma Hamilton,
January–February 1800 25

Napoleon Bonaparte to Josephine,
24 April 1796 28

Alexander II to Katya Dolgorukaya,
January 1868 30

Josef Stalin to Pelageya Onufrieva,
29 February 1912 33

Family

Elizabeth I to Mary I, 16 March 1554 37

Vilma Grünwald to Kurt Grünwald,
11 July 1944 40

Kadashman-Enlil to Amenhotep III,
c.1370 BC 41

Oliver Cromwell to Valentine Walton,
4 July 1644 43

Toussaint L'Ouverture to Napoleon,
12 July 1802 46

Alexander I to his sister Catherine,
20 September 1805 48

Charles I to Charles II,
29 November 1648 49

Svetlana Stalina to her father, Josef Stalin,
mid-1930s 52

Augustus to Caius Caesar,
23 September AD 2 53

Joseph II to his brother Leopold II,
4 October 1777 53

Rameses the Great to Ḫattušili III, 1243 BC . . . 55

Creation

Michelangelo to Giovanni da Pistoia, 1509 . . . 59

Wolfgang Amadeus Mozart to his cousin
Marianne, 13 November 1777 60

Honoré de Balzac to Ewelina Hánska,
19 June 1836 64

Pablo Picasso to Marie-Thérèse Walter,
19 July 1939 65

John Keats to Fanny Brawne,
13 October 1819 67

T. S. Eliot to George Orwell,
13 July 1944 69

Courage

Sarah Bernhardt to
Mrs. Patrick Campbell, 1915 75

Fanny Burney to her sister Esther,
22 March 1812 76

David Hughes to his parents,
21 August 1940 82

Discovery

Ada Lovelace to Andrew Crosse,
c.16 November 1844. 89

Wilbur Wright to the Smithsonian
Institution, 30 May 1899 91

John Stevens Henslow to Charles Darwin,
24 August 1831. 93

Between Ferdinand and Isabella, King and
Queen of Castile and Aragon, to Christopher
Columbus, 30 March 1493 and 29 April 1493. . 95

Tourism

Anton Chekhov to Anatoly Koni,
16 January 1891 105

Gustave Flaubert to Louis Bouilhet,
15 January 1850. 109

War

Peter the Great to Catherine I,
27 June 1709. 115

Napoleon to Josephine, 3 December 1805 116

Dwight D. Eisenhower to all Allied
troops, 5 June 1944. .117

Catherine, Duchess of Oldenburg, to her
brother Alexander I, 3 September 1812 118

Philip II to the Duke of Medina Sidonia,
1 July 1588 119

Harun al-Rashid to Nikephoros I, AD 802 . . 120

Rasputin to Nicholas II, 17 July 1914 121

Blood

Paiankh to Nodjmet, c.1070 BC 125

Vladimir Lenin to the Bolsheviks
of Penza, 11 August 1918 125

Josef Stalin to Kliment Voroshilov,
3 July 1937 126

Mao Zedong to the Red Guards
of Tsinghua University Middle School,
1 August 1966 127

Josip Broz Tito to Josef Stalin, 1948 129

Destruction

Theobald von Bethmann–Hollweg
to Count Leopold Berchtold, 6 July 1914 133

Harry Truman to Irv Kupcinet,
5 August 1963 135

Disaster

Pliny the Younger to Tacitus,
c.AD 106–107 141

Voltaire to M. Tronchin,
24 November 1755 146

Friendship

Captain A. D. Chater to his mother,
Christmas 1914 151

Mark Antony to Octavian
(later Augustus), c.33 BC 154

Between Karl Marx and Friedrich Engels,
July 1862–November 1864 155

Franklin D. Roosevelt
to Winston Churchill, 11 September 1939 ... 162

Adolf Hitler to Benito Mussolini,
21 June 1941 163

Between Prince Potemkin
and Catherine the Great, c.1774 170

Folly

Georg von Hülsen
to Emil von Görtz, 1892 175

The Marquis de Sade "to the stupid
villains who torment me," 1783 176

Between Empress Alexandra and
Nicholas II, 1916 178

Decency

Maria Theresa to Marie Antoinette,
30 July 1775 185

Mahatma Gandhi to Adolf Hitler,
24 December 1940.....................187

Abraham Lincoln to Ulysses S. Grant,
13 July 1863 190

John Profumo to Harold Macmillan,
5 June 1963..............................191

Jacqueline Kennedy to Nikita Khrushchev,
1 December 1963 193

Babur to his son Humayun,
11 January 1529 195

Émile Zola to Félix Faure,
13 January 1898 196

Lorenzo the Magnificent to his son
Giovanni de Medici,
23 March 1492 201

Liberation

Emmeline Pankhurst to the
Women's Social and Political Union,
10 January 1913 207

Rosa Parks to Jessica Mitford,
26 February 1956 209

Nelson Mandela to Winnie Mandela,
2 April 1969 211

Abram Hannibal to Peter the Great,
5 March 1722 214

Between Simón Bolívar, Manuela Sáenz,
and James Thorne, 1822–1823 215

Fate

Oscar Wilde to Robert Ross,
28 February 1895 221

Between Alexander Hamilton
and Aaron Burr, June 1804 222

Anonymous to Lord Monteagle,
October 1605 229

Babur to Humayun, 25 December 1526 231

Nikita Khrushchev
to John F. Kennedy, 24 & 26 October 1962 . . . 234

Alexander Pushkin
to Jacob von Heeckeren, 25 January 1837 239

Power

Stalin to Valery Mezhlauk, April 1930 245

Winston Churchill to Franklin D.
Roosevelt, 20 May 1940 246

Between Richard I and Saladin,
October–November 1191 247

Arthur James Balfour to Lord Rothschild,
2 November 1917 248

George H. W. Bush to Bill Clinton,
20 January 1993 250

Niccolò Machiavelli to Francesco Vettori,
3 August 1514 251

Henry VII to his "good friends," July 1485 253

John Adams to Thomas Jefferson,
20 February 1801 254

Between the Duke of Marlborough,
Queen Anne, and Sarah, Duchess
of Marlborough, 13 August 1704 255

Donald J. Trump to Kim Jong Un,
24 May 2018 257

Downfall

Abd al-Rahman III to his sons, AD 961. . . . 261

Simon Bar Kokhba to Yeshua, c.AD 135 262

Ammurapi to the king of Alashiya,
c.1190 BC 263

Aurangzeb to his son
Muhammed Azam Shah, 1707 264

Simón Bolívar to Juan José Flores,
9 November 1830. 265

Goodbye

Leonard Cohen to Marianne Ihlen,
July 2016 269

"Henriette" to Giacomo Casanova,
autumn 1749 270

Winston Churchill to his wife,
Clementine, 17 July 1915. 272

Nikolai Bukharin to Josef Stalin,
10 December 1937 274

Franz Kafka to Max Brod, June 1924 279

Walter Raleigh to his wife, Bess,
8 December 1603. 280

Alan Turing to Norman Routledge,
February 1952 284

Che Guevara to Fidel Castro, 1 April 1965 . . . 285

Robert Ross to More Adey,
14 December 1900 288

Lucrezia Borgia to Leo X, 22 June 1519 291

Hadrian to Antoninus Pius—
and to his soul, 10 July AD 138 292

Acknowledgments 295

Copyright Acknowledgments 297

Introduction

Dear Reader,

Nothing beats the immediacy and authenticity of a letter. We humans have an instinct to record feelings and memories that could be lost in time, and to share them. We desperately need to confirm relationships, ties of love or hate, for the world is never still and our lives are a series of beginnings and endings: in recording them on paper, we perhaps feel we can make them more real, almost eternal. Letters are the literary antidote to the ephemerality of life and, of course, the flimsy fitfulness of the Internet. Johann Wolfgang von Goethe, who reflected much on the magic of letters, thought them "the most significant memorial a person can leave." And those instincts are right: long after the protagonists are dead, letters live on. And in matters of politics, diplomacy, and war, a command or a promise must be documented. So many different things are achieved through the medium of letters, and we celebrate them all here.

There have been many collections of peculiar and funny letters, but these are chosen not just because they are entertaining but because they somehow changed human affairs, whether in war or peace, art or culture. They grant us a glimpse into fascinating lives, whether through the eyes of a genius, a monster, or an ordinary person. Here are letters from many cultures, traditions, lands, races: ancient Egypt and Rome to modern America, Africa, India, China, and Russia, where I have done a lot of my research and work—hence the presence here of many Russians, from Pushkin to Stalin. Here, among other things, are struggles for rights that we now regard as essential and orders for crimes we regard as intolerable. Here, too, are love letters and letters of power by empresses, actresses, tyrants, artists, composers, poets.

I have selected letters written by pharaohs three thousand years ago, preserved in forgotten libraries in fallen cities—and letters written this century. The letter certainly had a golden age: the five hundred years from the Middle Ages to the widespread use of the telephone in the 1930s, declining steeply in the 1990s with the arrival of the mobile telephone and the Internet. I saw it myself when I was researching in the Stalin archives. During the 1920s and 1930s, Stalin wrote long letters and notes to his entourage and to strangers, too, particularly when he was on holiday in the south, but when a secure telephone line was set up, his letters abruptly stopped.

Letters were naturally widely used by rulers and elites soon after writing itself developed: they are the ideal tool of management and much, much more. During the last three millennia, letters were the equivalent of today's newspapers, telephones, radio, television, email, texting, sexting, and blogging all put together. This anthology contains letters originally written in cuneiform, the ancient system of writing using the markings of a reed stylus on a flattened moist clay tablet and dried in the sun, utilized in the Middle East during the Bronze and Iron Ages. This collection also includes letters written on papyrus,

made with the pith of the papyrus plant, from the third millennium BC. And then there are letters written on parchment
or vellum—the tougher, dried animal skin—until paper was
created in China around 200 BC and gradually brought across
central Asia to Europe. There, its cheaper and easier manufac-
ture finally made it ever more convenient, available, and afford-
able from the fifteenth century onward. Letter-writing reached
a climax between the fifteenth and early twentieth centuries
not just because of the availability of paper but also because of
the ease of travel and distribution by courier and the development of post.

Letter writing was also more than practical—it was part of a
new state of order, of law and contract, responsible government,
accountable finance, and public morality. Above all, it was a new
state of mind with fresh ideas and modern visions of how to
live, an appreciation of privacy as well as a medium of promotion, and a growing sense of international society and personal
consciousness.

Some letters were intended to act as publicity; some were to
remain absolutely secret. Their variety of usage is one of the joys
of a collection like this. The vast majority of letters concerned
mundane practicalities of little interest—ordering goods, paying bills, arranging meetings. At the height of letter writing
as art and tool, literate people spent many hours a day at their
desks, sometimes in failing light, writing obsessively. Catherine
the Great self-deprecatingly called herself a "graphomaniac"
(she also called herself a "plantomaniac" for her love of garden-
ing) and the only way to run an empire, a war, a state was to
do so by frenzied letter writing. It was a way for the writers
to project their existence beyond their room, their house, vil-
lage, country to reach other worlds and distant dreams. It was a
physically exhausting duty *and* a pastime; emails and texts are
much less arduous to produce, but they are perhaps too easy, so

informal that we don't respect the power of the words themselves, though of course brevity, speed, and excitement make texting as addictive as it is essential in all modern lives. Until the early twentieth century, few people, even heads of state, had offices to assist them with their vast correspondence, and most of them answered and sealed (for security, partly) their own letters—including letter writers who figure in this book, such as Lincoln, Catherine, and Nicholas II, who actually stamped his own letters.

Of course, letter writers don't always tell the truth in their letters, and there can be an editing process in the choice of which letters they destroy and which they preserve. But either way, a letter reflects a single moment in time and experience—what Goethe called "the immediate breath of life." Many bonfires of letters were lit to destroy evidence of secret deals and forbidden loves. Such literary infernos happened frequently in Victorian and Edwardian families after the deaths of grandees—including in my own. But to destroy a letter, Goethe thought, even out of discretion, was destroying life itself.

History writing—like contemporary journalism—is full of gossip, guesswork, mythology, lies, misunderstandings, and calumnies. When we read a tabloid newspaper or a gossip site, we know that perhaps half of what we read is false: the joy of private letters is that they are the real thing. We are not depending on gossip: we can hear the authentic words. This is the way Stalin spoke to his henchmen, the way Hurrem talked lovingly to Suleiman the Magnificent, or Frida Kahlo to Diego Rivera. And then of course there are Mozart's outrageously scatological letters to his cousin Marianne.

These letters fall into various types. First: public letters. Mao Zedong launches the Cultural Revolution with a letter to students ordering them to attack their superiors; Balfour promises a Jewish homeland; Émile Zola's letter "J'Accuse!" confronts France about its racism and anti-Semitism. In the twenty-first century, I am afraid such a protest feels horribly contemporary—and absolutely necessary in our new venomous age of anti-Semitism on both sides of the Atlantic, not just from the right but increasingly, particularly in Britain, from the mainstream socialist left, a vile strain leading straight back to Stalin's anti-Semitic purges. But it also goes further back: Marxism is in fashion again. I have added some priceless letters between the two creators of Marxism, Karl Marx and Friedrich Engels, whose vicious and shameless racism and anti-Semitism may surprise those who regard them as selfless and noble campaigners for ordinary decency and equality. Far from it: their letters are peppered with words like *nigger* and *Yid* as well as reflections on the Jewish genitalia of their rival Lassalle. These may shock some readers.

In the centuries before the popularity of the press, many letters were designed to be copied out and widely distributed in society. Thus the public letters of great correspondents such as Voltaire and Catherine the Great were enjoyed in literary salons across Europe. Similarly with another sort of official letter: the announcement of a military victory or defeat. Even at the end of battles, when the fields were strewn with bodies quivering and shattered, exhausted generals would sit down in ruined cottages or at makeshift open-air desks to write letters throughout the night, announcing their victories to the world. After the victories of Poltava, Austerlitz, and Blenheim, Peter the Great, Napoleon, and Marlborough announced their news to the world—though they also boasted privately to their lovers and wives. "Come and celebrate with me!" writes Peter the Great to his wife.

Until recently, all negotiations or commands, particularly political or military ones, would be borne in letters *not* to be read by the public. In this book is Rameses the Great's disdainful note to the Hittite king Ḫattušili III. A millennium after that, Mark Antony writes to Octavian (the future emperor Augustus) to complain that his "screwing" Cleopatra is not politically significant—even though it clearly is. Leap a millennium again: Saladin and Richard the Lionheart negotiate to partition the Holy Land. Then forward another five hundred years: Philip II is ordering his admiral Medina Sidonia to command the Armada against England—even though the latter believes the enterprise will fail. Another four centuries and we are admiring Lincoln's generosity of spirit in a letter to General Grant. And there is no more important correspondence in the twentieth century than that between Roosevelt and Churchill during the desperate months of 1940. On the night before he invades Soviet Russia, Hitler reveals his motives in a letter to his ally Mussolini at the height of his hubristic swagger. And there's one letter here that was never sent: Eisenhower's draft addressed to the troops in case D-Day failed.

Then there is a special sort of letter that is both political and personal—and these are especially relevant in autocracies, where the intimate life of the ruler is political. As we can see in many of the new autocracies of the twenty-first century, when the ruler is absolute, everything personal is political. Henry VIII's love letter to Anne Boleyn and James I's to his handsome male favorite, the Duke of Buckingham, are of political importance— the ruler's amorous preferences guide national government. The repulsive entertainments, usually involving anuses and sausages, laid on for Kaiser Wilhelm II by his courtiers reveal the coarse incompetence that threatened European peace. Catherine the Great and Prince Potemkin, lovers as well as political partners, are passionate romantics yet clear-eyed politicians. Among their letters are some, ten to fifteen pages long, that discuss every aspect of power—diplomacy, war, finance, personnel. But they also cover domestic matters—art-collecting, building houses, their sexual affairs, and of course their health: no eighteenth-century letter is complete without a discussion of hemorrhoids. But their short love letters resemble modern emails or texts. Letters like these were never meant to be read by anyone but the recipients, but most were kept after their deaths. Potemkin died on a wild steppe in Moldova, gripping a packet of Catherine's letters wrapped in a ribbon, weeping as he read them.

Such *really* private correspondence celebrates love and sex, but these were letters that their writers kept under lock and key. Alexander II and his mistress (later wife) Katya exchange the most erotic letters ever written by a head of state. At the time they would have presumed that no one would ever see them— yet here we are, reading the letters of Vita Sackville-West and Virginia Woolf; Napoleon and Josephine; Emma Hamilton and Horatio Nelson. Balzac's correspondence with his Polish fan, the beautiful Countess Hánska, is so fervent, they fall in love before they meet—just by the power of letters. Anaïs Nin's correspondence with Henry Miller is so ablaze with sexuality, so awash with lubricity, it almost tastes of carnality. "More than kisses," wrote John Donne, "letters mingle souls." And bodies.

Naturally I have chosen intimate letters of pain as well as pleasure, of the end of love as well as the beginning: one of the most remarkable and little known is Thomas Jefferson's "conversation" between his Head and his Heart, sent to his young mistress who is leaving him. It must be one of the most brilliant analyses of the craziness of love ever written—and the acuity is not surprising, because this is the author of the American Declaration of Independence.

Similarly, Simón Bolívar tries to end his affair with the fabulous Manuela Sáenz. The married beauty "Henriette," returning to her husband, breaks the heart of the quintessential womanizer Casanova. Just before his own death, Leonard Cohen wishes farewell to his dying lover who inspired his greatest songs, including "So Long, Marianne." My favorite goodbye is the letter of the triumphant caliph of Islamic Spain, Abd-al Rahman III, who reflects on his deathbed that, out of fifty years of glory, he has enjoyed just fourteen days of happiness. Few letters are more heartbreaking than Alan Turing's agony over the persecution of his homosexuality. And of course there is the unbearable horror of a rare goodbye letter from wife to husband within the death camps of the Holocaust.

Some of these letters recount great events or spectacles—Columbus reports to his monarchs on the "discovery" of America; the Battle of Britain is recounted in a young pilot's letter to his parents, which is especially poignant because the pilot is killed soon afterward; Chekhov observes the suffering of the desperate criminals of Sakhalin; Pliny sees the destruction of Pompeii; Voltaire reflects on the Lisbon earthquake of 1755.

A subset of what we might call tourism tells of sexual adventures in interesting places, a popular type of letter in the eighteenth and nineteenth centuries, when the modern experience of travel as leisure expanded from the Grand Tours of wealthy aristocrats to middle-class travel by train, shrinking the world in a way never before achieved: Chekhov and Flaubert cheerfully describe encounters with Japanese prostitutes and Egyptian youths in beautiful prose.

Then there are letters of family, where we witness the intimate relationships of great men with their children, such as these two Mughal emperors: Babur advises his son on tolerance, and Aurangzeb writes to his son from his deathbed as his empire falls apart. As he awaits his own trial, Charles I tells his son how to be a king. Empress Maria Theresa warns her daughter Queen Marie Antoinette that her arrogance will destroy her. Or the other way around: Svetlana Stalina plays at being the dictator and gives orders to her father—including one to ban homework in the entire Soviet Union for a year. There is also the awkwardness of families, which among royalty is magnified to epic proportions. The future Queen Elizabeth I begs for her life from her sister Queen "Bloody" Mary. Joseph II comes to Paris as sex adviser to his sister Marie Antoinette, when Louis XVI is unable to consummate their marriage.

The anonymous warning of the Gunpowder Plot is itself decisive in defeating the conspiracy—it changes history at a stroke. Rasputin in his letter to Nicholas II tries to stop the First World War breaking out, but fails. Some of the letters are themselves orders to kill: Stalin's notes encourage his secret policemen to execute "enemies" who are actually innocent, and Lenin frenziedly orders executions of random victims. Three thousand years ago, an Egyptian ruler tells his wife to murder two junior officials and "disappear" their bodies. One of my favorites is Tito's laconic note to Stalin, threatening to send an assassin if Stalin tries to kill him again.

One special category covers *self*-destruction: Oscar Wilde receives the insulting letter from his lover's father calling him a "Somdomite"; Alexander Hamilton and Alexander Pushkin write their way toward the duels that kill them. Another particular species of letter is the last goodbye: for instance, Sir Walter Raleigh's letter to his wife before his execution. Emperor Hadrian, realizing he is dying, writes to his adopted son and successor Antoninus Pius. Bolívar, ailing and exhausted, damns the Americas. Kafka orders his works destroyed. And it is not just Kafka who doubts the value of his works: another theme is the torment and disappointment of creativity seen in such letters as Keats's on love and death; Michelangelo's stress as he paints the Sistine Chapel; or T. S. Eliot turning down George Orwell's new novel *Animal Farm*.

Here you will also read timeless letters that tell of the brave struggles for freedom in the modern era, such as the liberation of slaves, votes for women, and African American civil rights. Toussaint L'Ouverture, who has led the Haitian slave revolt against the French that leads to the first independent black republic of the Americas, now begs for his family's life. Nelson Mandela tells his wife, Winnie, how to live with hope, even inside a prison cell. Rosa Parks challenges racial segregation in Alabama. Abram Hannibal, a slave captured, probably, in West Africa, then sold to the slave markets of Istanbul and on to the Russian tsar, becomes the first black general in Europe. Gifted women defy their shackles: Ada Lovelace writes about her love of science; Fanny Burney and Manuela Sáenz defy the necessity of boring, male-centered marriage; Emmeline Pankhurst defends violent action in order to win the vote for women.

Email and the telephone may have ended the golden age of letters, but they have kept their power—for example, in diplomacy. In 2018, when President Donald Trump cancels his planned Singapore summit with the young and murderous North Korean dictator Kim Jong Un, he does so in a very Trumpian letter. It sparks an energetic correspondence. The summit takes place in Singapore after all. A few days later, on 6 July, Chairman Kim writes to Trump: "The significant first meeting with Your Excellency was indeed the start of a meaningful journey." Trump soon went further, boasting to a rally about his North Korean epistolary affair: "I was being really tough and so was he. We would go back and forth. And then we fell in love, okay? No, really—he wrote me beautiful letters, and they're great letters." Whatever the future of North Korean nuclear weapons, this at least proves the emotional and political power of the letter. While on the subject of the new brazen, vicious age of authoritarian swagger, ruthless bombast, and vicious hostility in public life, personified by Trump's presidency, I have added to this paperback the charming, elegant letter left by President George H. W. Bush (who had called for a "kinder, gentler" politics) for his successor, Bill Clinton, in the

Oval Office: it neatly and warmly puts aside petty insecurity and political malice to celebrate their shared American ideal. That's a sentiment sadly missing today.

Letters are returning to favor among those looking to be more discreet in their communication. Politicians, spies, criminals, and lovers have all learned, many the hard way, that emails and texts can be read and exposed; they are never destroyed. But they often vanish. Their impermanence makes them unsatisfying as a medium. They make life feel more transient while letters make it feel more enduring. Even the most heavily encrypted messages can be decrypted. Intelligence services like the CIA, GCHQ, or FSB, aided by renegade ghostly armies of plundering freelance hackers, are harvesting vast caches of messages. For this reason, people are starting to use pen and paper again, especially in government: letters can be preserved, but ironically they are safer, because they exist only once and can be physically destroyed. Top Russian officials now tell me that in the Kremlin today, all affairs of any importance are conducted by letter and note, on old-fashioned paper, with traditional ink or lead, nib or ballpoint, dispatched by loyal courier. No more sleek electronic devices! We should take note: no one knows like the Kremlin court of President Putin, that crenelated hive of cyber espionage, how insecure and dangerous are those easy texts and swift emails. Yet, as this anthology shows, letters often have a much longer life than their writers ever imagined.

I hope the readers of this collection wonder at the bravery, beauty, and visceral authenticity of these letters. While the surfer of the Internet feels more alone than ever amid invisible millions, the writer of a single letter to a correspondent is never lonely. Lord Byron, whose daughter Ada appears in this anthology, understood this when he mused that "letter writing is the only device combining solitude and good company," for the letter writer is enriched by the sensation of warmth that someone far away will soon share his or her sentiments. May it encourage *you* to write your own letters, inspired by the brilliance of these examples of the art.

Yours sincerely,
Simon Sebag Montefiore
May 2019

P.S. I hope you may also enjoy the companion volume of this book: *Voices of History: Speeches That Changed the World.*

P.P.S. In some cases, where the texts are too long, the detail too obscure, or the sex too repetitive, I have edited letters for the ease of the reader. Also, I have used the regnant names for all ruling monarchs, even if they were not yet sovereigns at the time of writing. This is to make it easy to recognize them: Elizabeth I was a princess of dubious prospects when she wrote the Tide Letter to Queen Mary—but the letter appears in the table of contents as "Elizabeth I to Mary I." Apologies if this bothers anyone.

Love

Henry VIII to Anne Boleyn, May 1528

This is one of the love letters that changed history. Henry was the second son of Henry VII, who had seized the throne for his newfangled Tudor dynasty in 1485. Only the death of his elder brother Prince Arthur brought Henry VIII to the throne, in 1509. Arthur left a young widow, Catherine of Aragon, daughter of the Spanish monarchs. On his accession, Henry suddenly decided to marry Catherine. Now, almost twenty years into their marriage, the king desperately needed a male heir. So far, only a daughter, Mary, had survived. After an affair with a young courtier named Mary Boleyn, he started to notice her sister, Anne, a lady-in-waiting to the queen. By 1528 Henry is in love with Anne Boleyn, eleven years younger than him. Although it is unlikely that their love affair has yet been consummated, he is already utterly enraptured by her. She is resisting his attempts at seduction. Her mix of chastity, sophistication, her ambition to marry the king and not be seduced like her sister, and her cool, haughty allure intensify Henry's fervor. Her personality makes him doubt her love—"I hope on yours also"—but later he would bitterly resent her wiles and take a terrible revenge.

Henry's love dovetailed with his conviction that his entire marriage to Catherine was incestuous and that divine displeasure was the cause of his lack of sons. He therefore ordered his ministers to secure an annulment from the pope. But the

Catholic Church would deny Henry's wishes in his Great Matter, which would lead to England's decisive break with Rome and the establishment of the Church of England; and in turn this allowed him to marry Anne in 1532. When Anne produced a daughter, the future Elizabeth I, but no sons, Henry turned on her: she was executed in 1536.

> My mistress and friend: I and my heart put ourselves in your hands, begging you to have them suitors for your good favor, and that your affection for them should not grow less through absence. For it would be a great pity to increase their sorrow since absence does it sufficiently, and more than ever I could have thought possible reminding us of a point in astronomy, which is, that the longer the days are the farther off is the sun, and yet the more fierce. So it is with our love, for by absence we are parted, yet nevertheless it keeps its fervor, at least on my side, and I hope on yours also: assuring you that on my side the ennui of absence is already too much for me: and when I think of the increase of what I must needs suffer it would be well nigh unbearable for me were it not for the firm hope I have and as I cannot be with you in person, I am sending you the nearest possible thing to that, namely, my picture set in a bracelet, with the whole device which you already know. Wishing myself in their place when it shall please you. This by the hand of
>
> *Your loyal servant and friend*
> H. Rex

Frida Kahlo to Diego Rivera, undated

Frida Kahlo's love letters to her husband, the painter Diego Rivera, are filled with the bold colors and wild passions of her art—and her life. Born of a German father and a Mexican mother in 1907, she was almost crippled by polio and was then terribly injured in a near-fatal bus accident in 1927. An iron rod had penetrated her uterus. She spent three months in a full-body cast and endured thirty operations and a lifetime of pain. While recovering, she started to paint and encountered Diego, already famous; both were leftists and they met through the Communist Party. Diego became her artistic mentor. Rivera had lived in Paris, traveled in Italy, and evolved his own style of murals, bold in color, his figures almost Aztec in their simplicity, all telling the history of Mexico and its revolution. Diego and Frida became lovers: he was forty-two, she twenty.

Kahlo and Rivera married in 1929, but the marriage was tempestuous. He was foul tempered and an enthusiastic womanizer, and she had affairs with men, including the Russian revolutionary leader in exile Leon Trotsky, as well as with women such as the French-American singer and dancer Josephine Baker. Neither her health problems nor the conservative Catholicism of much of Mexican society prevented her developing her artistic vision, her elaborate colorful costumes showing her mixed-race heritage, her liberated love life. Kahlo's dramatic artistic style, a flamboyant mix of fantastical and realistic, magical and folk, was inspired by both Mexico itself and her own extraordinary life. All of this is revealed in her letters to Rivera, in which physical love and emotional turbulence are often expressed in the colors of a painter: "the silent life giver of worlds, what is most important is the nonillusion. morning breaks, the friendly reds, the big blues, hands full of leaves, noisy birds, fingers in the

hair, pigeons' nests a rare understanding of human struggle simplicity of the senseless song the folly of the wind in my heart =
don't let them rhyme girl = sweet xocolatl [chocolate] of ancient
Mexico, storm in the blood that comes in through the mouth—
convulsion, omen, laughter and sheer teeth needles of pearl, for
some gift on a seventh of July, I ask for it, I get it, I sing, sang,
I'll sing from now on our magic—lo." She describes their love
in terms of Mexican landscape and even fruit: "it was the thirst
of many years restrained in your body. . . . There was all manner
of fruits in the juice of your lips, the blood of pomegranate, the
horizon of the mammee and the purified pineapple. I pressed
you against my breast and the prodigy of your form penetrated
my book through the tips of my fingers. Smell of oak essence,
memories of walnut, green breath of ash tree. Horizon and
landscapes, I trace them with a kiss. . . . I penetrate the sex
of the whole earth, her heat chars me and my entire body is
rubbed by the freshness of the tender leaves."

They divorced in 1939. For a long time, she was known
mainly as Diego's wife—but now the paintings of Frida and the
huge, exuberant murals of her husband form the national art of
Mexico. As for their volcanic relationship, she put it best: "only
one mountain can know the core of another mountain."

Diego:
    Nothing compares to your hands, nothing like the
green-gold of your eyes. My body is filled with you
for days and days. you are the mirror of the night. the
violent flash of lightning. the dampness of the earth.
The hollow of your armpits is my shelter. my fingers
touch your blood. All my joy is to feel life spring from
your flower-fountain that mine keeps to fill all the
paths of my nerves which are yours.

Thomas Jefferson to Maria Cosway,
12 October 1786

He is the American ambassador to Paris. She is "a golden-haired, languishing Anglo-Italian, graceful . . . and highly accomplished, especially in music." He is forty-three, she is twenty-seven. He is a widower, she is married. Jefferson, born in Virginia, was a wealthy landowner who, in 1776, had drafted the Declaration of Independence of the new nation of America. Born near Florence in 1759, Maria Cosway was the daughter of an expatriate English innkeeper and the wife of an eccentric painter. In Paris, during autumn 1786, Maria and Jefferson have spent an intense month in each other's company.

When she leaves, Jefferson writes her this extraordinary letter in which one of the reigning intellects of Western history applies himself to the dilemma of love, to heartbreak, and to human nature. To be in love, to drink the elixir of loving, he argues, is worth the inevitable heartbreak. And America would not have been liberated without the passion of the heart. His conclusion? "We have no rose without its thorn." They never meet again, but correspond for the rest of their lives. Soon after Maria leaves, Jefferson is joined in Paris by his daughter and her mixed-race slave companion, Sally Heming, sixteen, with whom Jefferson begins a relationship that would produce at least five children. In 1790, Jefferson returned home to become the first secretary of state in President Washington's cabinet and was elected the third president in 1801. Here is this very special letter that expresses the agonies and dilemmas of any man or woman unsuitably in love.

Seated by my fireside solitary and sad, the following dialogue took place between my Head and my Heart.

Head. Well, friend, you seem to be in a pretty trim.

Heart. I am indeed the most wretched of all earthly beings. Overwhelmed with grief, every fiber of my frame distended beyond its natural powers to bear, I would willingly meet whatever catastrophe should leave me no more to feel or to fear.

Head. These are the eternal consequences of your warmth and precipitation. This is one of the scrapes into which you are ever leading us. You confess your follies indeed: but you still hug and cherish them; and no reformation can be hoped, where there is no repentance.

Heart. Oh my friend! This is no moment to upbraid my foibles. I am rent into fragments by the force of my grief! If you have any balm, pour it into my wounds: if none, do not harrow them by new torments. Spare me in this awful moment! At any other I will attend with patience to your admonitions.

Head. On the contrary I never found that the moment of triumph with you was the moment of attention to my admonitions. While suffering under your follies you may perhaps be made sensible of them, but, the paroxysm over, you fancy it can never return. Harsh therefore as the medicine may be, it is my office to administer it. . . .

Heart. May heaven abandon me if I do! . . .

Head. I wished to make you sensible how imprudent it is to place your affections, without reserve, on objects you must so soon lose and whose loss when it comes

must cost you such severe pangs. Remember the last
night. You knew your friends were to leave Paris today.
This was enough to throw you into agonies. All night
you tossed us from one side of the bed to the other.
No sleep, no rest. . . . To avoid these eternal distresses,
to which you are forever exposing us, you must learn
to look forward before each step which may interest
our peace. Everything in this world [is] a matter of
calculation. Advance then with caution, the balance
in your hand. Put into one scale the pleasures which
any object may offer; but put fairly into the other the
pains which are to follow, and see which preponderates.
The making [of] an acquaintance is not a matter of
indifference. When a new one is proposed to you, view
it all round. Consider what advantages it presents, and
what inconveniences it may expose you. Do not bite
at the bait of pleasure till you know there is no hook
beneath it. The art of life is the art of avoiding pain: and
he is the best pilot who steers clearest of the rocks and
shoals with which he is beset. Pleasure is always before
us; but misfortune is at our side: while running after
that, this arrests us. The most effectual means of being
secure against pain is to retire within ourselves, and to
suffice for our own happiness. . . .

Heart. And what more sublime delight than to mingle
tears with one whom the hand of heaven hath smitten!
To watch over the bed of sickness, and to beguile its
tedious and its painful moments! To share our bread
with one to whom misfortune has left none! This world
abounds indeed with misery; to lighten its burdens
we must divide it with one another. . . . When nature
assigned us the same habitation, she gave us over it a

divided empire. To you she allotted the field of science, to me that of morals. When the circle is to be squared, or the orbit of a comet to be traced; when the arch of greatest strength, or the solid of least resistance is to be investigated, take you the problem: it is yours; nature has given me no cognizance of it. In like manner in denying to you the feelings of sympathy, of benevolence, of gratitude, of justice, of love, of friendship, she has excluded you from their control. To these she has adapted the mechanism of the heart. Morals were too essential to the happiness of man to be risked on the uncertain combinations of the head. She laid their foundation therefore in sentiment, not science. That she gave to all, as necessary to all: this to a few only, as sufficing with a few. I know indeed that you pretend authority to the sovereign control of our conduct in all its parts: and a respect for your grave saws and maxims, a desire to do what is right, has sometimes induced me to conform to your counsels. . . . If our country, when pressed with wrongs at the point of a bayonet had been governed by its heads instead of its hearts, where should we have been now? Hanging on a gallows as high as Haman's. You began to calculate and to compare wealth and numbers: we threw up a few pulsations of our warmest blood: we supplied enthusiasm against wealth and numbers: we put our existence to the hazard, when the hazard seemed against us, and we saved our country: justifying at the same time the ways of Providence, whose precept is to do always what is right, and leave the issue to him. In short, my friend, as far as my recollection serves me, I do not know that I ever did a good thing on your suggestion, or a dirty one without it. I do forever then

disclaim your interference in my province. Fill paper
as you please with triangles and squares: try how many
ways you can hang and combine them together. . . .
We are not immortal ourselves, my friend; how can
we expect our enjoyments to be so? We have no rose
without its thorn; no pleasure without alloy. It is the
law of our existence; and we must acquiesce.

Catherine the Great to Prince Potemkin, c.19 March 1774

This is the letter that reveals one of the most successful romantic
partnerships and political alliances in all of history. Catherine
was brought to Russia as a young German princess to marry the
poxy heir to the throne, Grand Duke Peter, an inadequate bully
who made her life hell. She was clever, cultured, passionate, and
ambitious. Desperately lonely, she was supported personally
and politically by a series of lovers. When it had become clear
that her husband, as Emperor Peter III, was both a disastrous
tsar and a dangerous man, she overthrew him with the aid of
her lover, Orlov, and made herself Catherine II. Peter III was
strangled. In danger of being murdered herself, Catherine was
scarcely helped by Orlov. When their relationship foundered, his
replacement was an intellectual nonentity named Vasilchikov,
who made her even more unhappy. She needed the support of
an equal, and she knew Grigory Potemkin already. Brilliant,
flamboyant, and masterful, he was already in love with her.

Now she falls in love with him, knowing he has an intel-
lect as superb as hers. In their letters, they call each other "twin
souls," writing day and night. Sometimes her letters are like
texts: "Me love general, general love me," but their ambitions are
imperial. Physical passion dovetails with political acumen and

changes Russia's history: together they expand into Ukraine, annex Crimea, and found a Black Sea fleet as well as new cities from Odessa to Kherson.

In this letter, Catherine, nicknaming Potemkin "my hero," "a Cossack," and a Muslim Tatar (a "giaour"), admits that even at dawn, after a row in which she decides to break up, she cannot live without the charismatic Potemkin: she is overcome with love and lust—what has he done to the cleverest woman in Europe?

Darling, really now, I suppose you thought I wouldn't write to you today. You're quite mistaken, sir. I awoke at five o'clock, it's now after six—I should write to him [Vasilchikov]. But only so much as to speak the truth, and kindly take heed what sort of truth: I don't love you and don't want to see you anymore. You won't believe it, my love, but I can't abide you at all. Yesterday we chatted till twelve o'clock, and then he was sent away. Don't be angry—indeed, as if one couldn't do without him. The dearest thing of all that came from that conversation is that I learned what they say among themselves: no, they say, this is no Vasilchikov, this one she treats differently. And he is indeed worthy. No one is surprised, and the affair has been accepted as if they have long been expecting it. But no—everything must be otherwise. From my pinky to my heel and from these to the last hair on my head, I have issued a general prohibition today against showing you the least affection. And my love is being kept in my heart under lock and key. It's awful how cramped it is in there. With great difficulty it squeezes itself inside, so mind well—it might just pop out somewhere. Now see here, you are a reasonable man, could so few lines contain more madness? A flood of foolish words has sprung from my head. How you can enjoy spending time with such a deranged mind I do not know. Oh, Mister Potemkin, what strange miracle have you performed in so thoroughly deranging a head that earlier was considered by society to be one of the best in Europe?

It's time, high time indeed to start acting sensibly. It's shameful, it's bad, it's a sin for Catherine the Second to allow this mad passion to rule over her. Such foolhardiness will make you loathsome even to him. I'll begin repeating that last verse to myself often, and I hope this alone will be enough to lead me back onto the true path. But this won't be the final proof of your great power over me. It's time to stop or I'll scribble a complete sentimental metaphysics that will finally make you laugh, though this will be its sole benefit. Well, my nonsense, off you go to those places, those happy shores where my hero dwells. If, perchance, you don't find him still at home and are carried back to me, then I shall toss you directly into the fire and Grishenka won't see this extravagant behavior, in which, however, God knows, there is much love; but it would be much better if he didn't know of this.

Farewell, giaour, Muscovite, Cossack. I don't love you.

James I to George Villiers, Duke of Buckingham, 17 May 1620

This is a love letter from the married King James I to his adored male favorite. James had a history of intimate relationships with handsome young men. From the moment James saw George Villiers in 1614, aged twenty-one, he was dazzled by the youth's physical beauty, and he turned out to be intelligent, too, if not especially talented. Appointed the king's cupbearer, he was swiftly promoted all the way up the peerage to duke of Buckingham (1623)—and effectively chief minister as Lord High Admiral—making him the most hated man in the kingdom. James publicly kissed and caressed George, whom he lovingly called "Steenie" because St. Stephen had "the face of an angel," and he admitted in 1617 to the Council "you may be sure that I love the Earl of Buckingham more than anyone else. . . . I wish . . . not to have it thought to be a defect, for Jesus Christ did the same, and therefore I cannot be blamed. Christ had John, and I have George." There was probably some sexual relationship: Buckingham reminisced in a letter to James "whether you loved me now . . . better than at the time which I shall never forget at Farnham, where the bed's head could not be found between the master and his dog." James called Buckingham his wife: "God bless you, my sweet child and wife, and grant that ye may ever be a comfort to your dear father and husband." Remarkably, Buckingham also managed to become best friends with James's son and heir Charles I. He remained on top after James's death. But in 1628, he was assassinated by a disgruntled officer. In this letter written at the height of his power, James has helped him make a rich marriage to Lady Katherine Manners, but even after the wedding, he still praises Buckingham's "white teeth."

My only sweet and dear child,
    Thy dear dad sends thee his blessing this morning and also to his daughter. The Lord of Heaven send you a sweet and blithe wakening, all kind of comfort in

your sanctified bed, and bless the fruits thereof that
I may have sweet bedchamber boys to play me with,
and this is my daily prayer, sweet heart. When thou
risest, keep thee from importunity of people that may
trouble thy mind, that at meeting I may see thy white
teeth shine upon me, and so bear me comfortable
company in my journey. And so God bless thee,
hoping thou will not forget to read over again my
former letter.

James R.

Vita Sackville-West to Virginia Woolf,
21 January 1926

Vita Sackville-West was an aristocratic poet and novelist,
daughter of Lord Sackville. After she married the diplomat
Harold Nicolson in 1913 she continued to have love affairs with
women, and perhaps the greatest love of her life was with the
novelist Virginia Woolf. In February 1923, Woolf wrote in her
diary: "[Vita] is a practiced Sapphist & may . . . have an eye on
me, old though I am." Virginia, neé Stephens and married to
Leonard Woolf, was then forty-four, ten years older than Vita.
Virginia considered herself provincial and dowdy by comparison with Vita's flamboyant libertinism, as well as less successful
as a writer. Vita admired Virginia's "exquisite" writing. In this
unshowy love letter, Sackville-West, writing to Woolf from one
of her Italian retreats in early 1926, reassures her lover of her
affections, even though she has other lovers. The relationship
was over by 1928, but it inspired Woolf's novel *Orlando* which,
with its recognizable gender-switching protagonist, is in some
ways Virginia's love letter to Vita.

MILAN
THURSDAY, JANUARY 21, 1926

I am reduced to a thing that wants Virginia. I
composed a beautiful letter to you in the sleepless
nightmare hours of the night, and it has all gone: I
just miss you, in a quite simple desperate human way.
You, with all your undumb letters, would never write
so elementary a phrase as that; perhaps you wouldn't
even feel it. And yet I believe you'll be sensible of a
little gap. But you'd clothe it in so exquisite a phrase
that it would lose a little of its reality. Whereas with
me it is quite stark: I miss you even more than I could
have believed; and I was prepared to miss you a good
deal. So this letter is just really a squeal of pain. It is
incredible how essential to me you have become. I
suppose you are accustomed to people saying these
things. Damn you, spoiled creature; I shan't make you
love me any the more by giving myself away like
this—But oh my dear, I can't be clever and stand-offish
with you: I love you too much for that. Too truly. You
have no idea how stand-offish I can be with people
I don't love. I have brought it to a fine art. But you
have broken down my defenses. And I don't really
resent it. . . .

   Please forgive me for writing such a miserable letter.

V.

Between Suleiman the Magnificent
and Hurrem Sultan, c.1530s

These two love letters tell the story of the partnership of a slave girl and the most powerful monarch in the world. She was probably a blonde Russian priest's daughter, a Christian, who was captured and sold into the harem of the Ottoman sultan Suleiman the Magnificent, who ruled for forty-six years from 1520. She was obviously a remarkable character of force and intelligence. Although he had access to thousands of odalisques in the harem and already had a consort who had given him a son and heir, Prince Mustafa, Suleiman fell in love with Roxelana, giving her the new name Hurrem, "Delight," for her exuberance and "eyes full of mischief."

Ottoman padishahs wrote love poetry using noms de plume, and Suleiman, often away fighting the Hungarians or the Persians, wrote Hurrem poems under the name Muhibbi. Here is one of his verses that are still celebrated.

Suleiman to Hurrem

Throne of my lonely niche, my wealth, my love, my moonlight.
My most sincere friend, my confidante, my very existence, my Sultan
The most beautiful among the beautiful . . .
My springtime, my merry faced love, my daytime, my sweetheart, laughing leaf . . .
My plants, my sweet, my rose, the one only who does not distress me in this world . . .
My Istanbul, my Caraman, the earth of my Anatolia
My Badakhshan, my Baghdad, my Khorasan

My woman of the beautiful hair, my love of the slanted
brow, my love of eyes full of mischief . . .
I'll sing your praises always
I, lover of the tormented heart, Muhibbi of the eyes full of
tears, I am happy

Around 1521, Hurrem gave birth to a first son—the essential male heir. Suleiman ignored the restriction of one son to each concubine, and around 1533, he married her, breaking the precedent that sultans didn't wed concubines. Hurrem had the luck to give her emperor five sons and a daughter, mentioned in this letter. Most lived long lives—especially their beautiful and intelligent daughter Mihrimah, who became her father's trusted aide and the adviser to her brother Selim, too. Over the years, Hurrem proved a formidable politician, challenging the monarch's eldest son Mustafa, who was strangled on the orders of his father. Hurrem died in 1558, before Suleiman, but she managed to contrive the succession in 1566 of her son Selim. Hurrem's domed tomb stands next to Suleiman's in the Süleymaniye Mosque, Istanbul. Here is one of Hurrem's letters to Suleiman on campaign:

Hurrem to Suleiman

My Sultan, there is no limit to the burning anguish
of separation. Now spare this miserable one and do
not withhold your noble letters. Let my soul gain at
least some comfort from a letter. . . . When your noble
letters are read, your servant and son Mir Mehmed
and your slave and daughter Mihrimah weep and wail
from missing you. Their weeping has driven me mad,
it is as if we were in mourning. My Sultan, your son

Mir Mehmed and your daughter Mihrimah and Selim
Khan and Abdullah send you many greetings and rub
their faces in the dust at your feet.

Anaïs Nin to Henry Miller,
c.August 1932

Born in France in 1903 to Cuban parents, Anaïs Nin gave new
expression to female power, freedom, and eroticism as well
as to female suffering from male abuse. She kept diaries that
recorded her incestuous, abusive relationship with her father,
then as she grew up she celebrated her own sensibilities, literary,
emotional, and erotic. Living with her Scottish banker husband
Hugh Guiler in Paris in the 1930s, she was writing essays and
stories but putting her talent into her diaries.

The American writer Henry Miller, nicknamed "the gang-
ster author," was living hand-to-mouth in Paris while he com-
pleted the first of his erotic, ribaldly Rabelaisian, masculine
masterpieces, *Tropic of Cancer*. But both lived for writing—"at
the *core* of us is a writer, not a human being," Nin wrote. He
was thirty-nine, penniless, and married to his second wife, June
Smith, a fascinating, secretive beauty, when he came for lunch
at the Guilers'. He came alone—June was still in New York.

Nin, aged twenty-nine, first becomes obsessed with Miller
as a writer. When she meets his wife, June, the two women
have a short affair. Then Anaïs and Henry embark on their own
voyage of sex and literature. He admires her diary and stories;
she recognizes the greatness of his novels *Tropic of Cancer* and
Tropic of Capricorn, in which June appears as the femme fatale,
Mona/Mara. Nin and her husband paid for their publication.
Their affair was always adventurously erotic and also a cele-

bration of life. "He is a man who life makes drunk," she wrote, "like me." But after making love, they discussed books at length: "Henry used my love well, beautifully—he erected books with it."

Theirs is one of the best romantic correspondences—sexy, messy, uninhibited, poetical, beautifully written, unhinged: "Anaïs," he writes in the summer of 1932, "Here is the first woman with whom I can be absolutely sincere. . . . I mean I can never be absolutely loyal—it's not in me—I love women or life too much. . . . But laugh Anaïs. . . . I love to hear you laugh. You are the only woman who has had a sense of gaiety, a wise tolerance—no, more, you seem to urge me to betray you. I love you for that. And what makes you do that—love? Oh it is beautiful to love and to be free at the same time. . . . I love you laughingly. . . . Come here quickly and screw me. Shoot with me. Wrap you legs around me. Warm me." When *Tropic of Cancer* was published in 1934, Miller became famous and notorious for this and his Rosy Crucifixion trilogy. Anaïs became famous for her diaries and novels such as *A Spy in the House of Love*. Her erotic short stories *Delta of Venus* changed female eroticism when finally published posthumously in 1977. Their affair ended after ten years but they remained friends for life—and master letter writers. This letter catches the passion and the hatred of their ménage a trois—and Anaïs's generosity of spirit.

You are right, in one sense, when you speak of honesty.
An effort, anyway, with the usual human or feminine
retractions. To retreat is not feminine, male, or trickery.
It is a terror before utter destruction. What we analyze
inexorably, will it die? Will June die? Will our love
die, suddenly, instantaneously if you should make a

LOVE   21

caricature of it? Henry, there is danger in too much
knowledge. You have a passion for absolute knowledge.
That is why people will hate you.

And sometimes I believe your relentless analysis of
June leaves something out, which is your feeling for her
beyond knowledge, or in spite of knowledge. I often
see how you sob over what you destroy, how you want
to stop and just worship; and you do stop, and then
a moment later you are at it again with a knife, like a
surgeon.

What will you do after you have revealed all there is
to know about June? Truth. What ferocity in your quest
of it. You destroy and you suffer. In some strange way
I am not with you, I am against you. We are destined
to hold two truths. I love you and I fight you. And you,
the same. We will be stronger for it, each of us, stronger
with our love and our hate. When you caricature and
nail down and tear apart, I hate you. I want to answer
you, not with weak or stupid poetry but with a wonder
as strong as your reality. I want to fight your surgical
knife with all the occult and magical forces of the
world.

I want to both combat you and submit to you,
because as a woman I adore your courage, I adore
the pain it engenders, I adore the struggle you carry
in yourself, which I alone fully realize, I adore your
terrifying sincerity. I adore your strength. You are right.
The world is to be caricatured, but I know, too, how
much you can love what you caricature.

How much passion there is in you! It is that I feel in
you. I do not feel the savant, the revealer, the observer.
When I am with you, it is the blood I sense.

This time you are not going to awake from the
ecstasies of our encounters to reveal only the ridiculous
moments. No. You won't do it this time, because while
we live together, while you examine my indelible rouge
effacing the design of my mouth, spreading like blood
after an operation (you kissed my mouth and it was
gone, the design of it was lost as in a watercolor, the
colors ran); while you do that, I seize upon the wonder
that is brushing by (the wonder, oh, the wonder of
my lying under you), and I bring it to you, I breathe
it around you. Take it. I feel prodigal with my feelings
when you love me, feelings so unblunted, so new,
Henry, not lost in resemblance to other moments, so
much ours, yours, mine, you and I together, not any
man or any woman together.

What is more touchingly real than your room.
The iron bed, the hard pillow, the single glass. And all
sparkling like a Fourth of July illumination because
of my joy, the soft billowing joy of the womb you
inflamed. The room is full of the incandescence you
poured into me. The room will explode when I sit at the
side of your bed and you talk to me. I don't hear your
words: your voice reverberated against my body like
another kind of caress, another kind of penetration. I
have no power over your voice. It comes straight from
you to me. I could stuff my ears and it would find its
way into my blood and make it rise.

I am impervious to the flat visual attack of things.
I see your khaki shirt hung up on a peg. It is your shirt
and I could see you in it—you, wearing a color I detest.
But I see you, not the khaki shirt. Something stirs in
me as I look at it, and it is certainly the human you.

It is a vision of the human you revealing an amazing delicacy to me. It is your khaki shirt and you are the man who is the axis of my world now. I revolve around the richness of your being.

"Come closer to me, come closer. I promise you it will be beautiful."

You keep your promise.

Listen, I do not believe that I alone feel that we are living something new because it is new to me. I do not see in your writing any of the feelings you have shown me or any of the phrases you have used. When I read your writing, I wondered, What episode are we going to repeat?

You carry your vision, and I mine, and they have mingled. If at moments I see the world as you see it (because they are Henry's whores I love them), you will sometimes see it as I do.

Alexandra to Rasputin, 1909

All of Russia was gripped by the nature of the empress Alexandra's relationship with her confidant, Siberian peasant holy man, Grigory Rasputin. It was a fascination that, step by step, would destroy the monarchy's prestige.

From 1905 when they first meet him, Alexandra, her husband Tsar Nicholas II, and their children write regularly to Rasputin who gives them all advice and guidance. The tsarina believes that he has the power to stop the bleeding of her hemophiliac son Alexei. But as this letter shows, Rasputin is also essential to the tsar and tsarina as a combination of priest, psychiatrist, and adviser. They revere him as a Christ-like link to God and an authentic peasant who confirms their belief in the mystical connection between tsar and people. It is astonishing that this haughty, neurotic monarch, granddaughter of Queen Victoria, wishes to kiss his hands and sleep next to him, but contrary to popular belief, Alexandra was extremely prim: she had no sexual contact with Rasputin. He is, as she writes, "my beloved mentor." It is a reverence that endures to his murder in 1916 and beyond, to the murder of the Romanovs themselves in July 1918, when their bodies are still wearing keepsakes given to them by Rasputin.

It was a mark of Rasputin's lack of judgment that he allowed this letter to fall into the hands of a rival priest who deliberately leaked it to embarrass Rasputin and his royal patrons. When it was published, many thought it was too outrageous to be real. But it was genuine.

My beloved and unforgettable teacher, savior and mentor.
    How tiring it is for me to be without you. My soul is calm and I can rest only when you, my teacher, are seated next to me, and I kiss your hands and lay my head on your blessed shoulders. Oh, how easy things are for me then. Then I wish only for one thing— to fall asleep, fall asleep forever on your shoulders, in your embrace. Oh, what happiness it is just to feel your presence near me. Where are you? Whither have you flown? It's so difficult for me, such longing in my heart. . . . But you, my beloved mentor, don't say a word to Anya [Vyrubova, Alexandra's friend] about my sufferings without you. Anya is good, she is kind, she loves me, but don't tell her of my sorrow. Will you soon be here near me? Come soon. I am waiting for you and am miserable without you. Give me your holy blessing, and I kiss your blessed hands.
                    Loving you for all times. Mama.

Horatio Nelson to Emma Hamilton,
January–February 1800

Horatio Nelson had first met Emma, Lady Hamilton, beautiful former actress and wife of the super-rich British ambassador to the court of Naples, in the first years of the wars against Revolutionary France. When they met again, Nelson had become Britain's foremost naval hero and a physical wreck. He had already lost an eye ("I got a little hurt his morning") and had an arm amputated ("the sooner it's off the better") after being wounded in battle. Then in August 1798 he fought the Battle of the Nile—"Before this time tomorrow, I shall have gained a peerage or Westminster Abbey." Hit by shot on the forehead with a flap of skin obscuring his remaining eye, he said, "I am killed. Remember me to my wife." But the wound was light and he wiped out Napoleon Bonaparte's fleet, leaving the French general stranded in Egypt.

Afterward, he became a legend—Baron Nelson of the Nile and Duke of Bronte—and spent much time being lionized in the exotic city of Naples where he and Emma fell in love. Nelson was forty-two, a ruin of a man, and she was thirty-five and still beautiful. The lovers spent much time with her old husband, the ambassador Sir William Hamilton, a scandal that naturally reached the ears of Nelson's long-suffering wife Fanny and London society.

When peace was finally signed with France, Nelson and the Hamiltons went on a European cruise during which their daughter Horatia was conceived, returning to London in 1800. Emma was besieged with admirers, including the Prince Regent, and when Nelson grew jealous Hamilton wrote a rather unusual letter to him, insisting that his wife, in her infidelity to himself, was staying faithful to Nelson.

When the war started again in 1804, Nelson moved to confront the Franco-Spanish fleet, first writing a will ordering that Emma be granted "ample provision to maintain her rank in life," and that his "adopted daughter, Horatia Nelson Thompson . . . use in future the name of Nelson only." Nelson destroyed the Franco-Spanish fleet at Trafalgar but was shot dead by a French sniper. He was buried in St. Paul's Cathedral but his will was ignored: Emma died in penury ten years later. This blazingly ardent letter dates from the first days of their passion: ordered to report to his admiral at Livorno, every mile away from Emma is agony. Nelson has promised to not "sleep on shore"—lest he flirt with anyone else—and swears not even to enjoy pudding, until he makes love to her again. The "obstacles" are their spouses, Sir William Hamilton and Fanny Nelson.

> Separated from all I hold dear in this world what is the use of living if indeed such an existence can be called so, nothing could alleviate such a separation but the call of our Country but loitering time away with nonsense is too much. No separation no time my only beloved Emma can alter my love and affection for you, it is founded on the truest principles of honor, and it only remains for us to regret which I do with the bitterest anguish that there are any obstacles to our being united in the closest ties of this world's rigid rules, as we are in those of real love. Continue only to love your faithful Nelson as he loves his Emma. You are my guide I submit to you, let me find all my fond heart hopes and wishes with the risk of my life. I have been faithful to my word never to partake of any amusement: or to sleep on shore.

Thursday January 30th: we have been six days from
Leghorn and no prospect of our making a passage to
Palermo, to me it is worse than death. I can neither
eat nor sleep for thinking of you my dearest love,
I never touch even pudding you know the reason.
No I would starve sooner. My only hope is to find you
have equally kept your promises to me, for I never
made you a promise that I did not as strictly keep as
if made in the presence of heaven, but I rest perfectly
confident of the reality of your love and that you
would die sooner than be false in the smallest thing
to your own faithful Nelson who lives only for his
Emma.

    Friday, I shall run mad we have had a gale of wind
that is nothing but I am 20 Leagues farther from you
than yesterday noon. Was I master notwithstanding
the weather I would have been 20 Leagues nearer
but my Commander in Chief knows not what I feel
by absence. Last night I did nothing but dream of
you altho' I woke 20 times in the night. In one of
my dreams I thought I was at a large table. You was
not present, sitting between a Princess who I detest
and another, they both tried to seduce me and the
first wanted to take those liberties with me which
no woman in this world but yourself ever did, the
consequence was I knocked her down and in the
moment of bustle you came in and taking me in your
embrace whispered I love nothing but you my Nelson.
I kissed you fervently and we enjoy'd the height of
love. Ah Emma I pour out my soul to you. If you love
any thing but me you love those who feel not like
your N.

Sunday noon, fair Wind which makes me a little better
in hopes of seeing you my love my Emma is tomorrow,
just 138 miles distant, and I trust to find you like myself,
for no love is like mine toward you.

Napoleon Bonaparte to Josephine, 24 April 1796

Theirs is a love match. He is the young victorious general of
Revolutionary France; she is a Creole girl born in Martinique,
the widow of an aristocrat guillotined during the Terror of the
early 1790s. She became the mistress of Paul Barras, one of
the ruling Directors of France who then introduced her to his
rising general Napoleon, whom she married on 9 March 1796.
Afterward, Napoleon defeated France's enemies—the Austrians,
the Russians, the Prussians, the Egyptians—and himself seized
power in France. In 1804, he crowned himself and Josephine
emperor and empress. But he needed an heir and the marriage
had produced no children. He therefore divorced Josephine and
married Archduchess Marie Louise, Habsburg daughter of the
Emperor of Austria, with whom he had a son. When Napoleon lost his empire and went into exile in 1814, Josephine was
admired by all for enduring all these blows with her characteristic style—but she died just months later.

This letter finds her in Paris while General Bonaparte is fighting in Italy—just after their marriage, but already he is craving
her, tormented with jealousy. She is fashionable and chic, flirtatious and unfaithful; he is obsessional, controlling, and puppy-
ishly devoted, bombarding her with letters that praise, seduce,
threaten, whine, and boast in equal parts. He raves about her
body and her sexual technique, something called the "zigzag,"
begging her not to wash so he could smell her. As we read in this

letter, he always wants to kiss her on the heart as well as "lower down, much lower."

My brother will bring you this letter. I have the greatest love for him and I hope he will gain yours; he deserves it. Nature has given him a sweet and utterly good character; he is full of good qualities.

I am writing to Barras to get him appointed consul in some Italian port. He wants to live with his little wife far away from the hurly-burly and political affairs; I commend him to you.

I have your letters of the 16th and the 21st. There are many days when you don't write. What do you do, then?

No, my darling, I am not jealous, but sometimes worried. Come soon; I warn you, if you delay, you will find me ill.

Fatigue and your absence are too much.

Your letters are the joy of my days, and my days of happiness are not many.

Junot is bringing twenty-two flags to Paris. You must come back with him, do you understand?

Hopeless sorrow, inconsolable misery, sadness without end, if I am so unhappy as to see him return alone.

Adorable friend, he will see you, he will breathe in your temple; perhaps you will grant him the unique and perfect flavor of kissing your cheek, and I shall be alone and far, far away.

But you are coming, aren't you? You are going to be here beside me, in my arms, on my breast, on my mouth.

Take wing and come, come! But travel gently. The road is long, bad, tiring.

Suppose you had an accident, or fell ill; suppose fatigue—come gently, my adorable love, but I think of you often.

I have received a letter from Hortense [Josephine's daughter who would marry Napoleon's brother Louis, future king of Holland]. I will write to her. She is altogether charming. I love her and will soon send her the perfumes she wants.

Read Ossian's poem "Carthon" carefully, and sleep well and happily far from your good friend, but thinking of him.

A kiss on the heart, and one lower down, much lower!

B.

I don't know if you need money; you have never talked about your business matters. If so, you can ask my brother, who has 200 louis of mine.

Alexander II to Katya Dolgorukaya, January 1868

Alexander II's correspondence with Katya is probably the most explicit ever written by a political leader. But the letters are also poignant, passionate, and political. He is around forty years old, the most attractive of the Romanov emperors—a reformer who has just liberated the serfs—when he falls in love with a teenage girl about to leave school: Princess Ekaterina Dolgorukaya. One day in January 1865 they bump into each other in the park outside her boarding school minutes before a terrorist tries to assassinate the tsar. Alexander regards their love as sacredly sanctioned, her as a guardian angel. Bored with his prim wife and heartbroken after the death of his eldest son, Alexander finds himself under astonishing pressure as terrorists launch an assassination campaign against him. His consolation is Katya, with whom he shares the comfort of love and a mutually intense eroticism. In several letters a day, scrawled in French, they relish their sexual sessions together using the code word *bingerle* for sex.

In their letters, Alexander remembers the first time they met in secret: "I'll never forget what happened on the sofa in the mirrored room when we kissed on the mouth for the first time, and you made me go out while you removed your crinoline which was in our way and I was surprised to find you without your pantaloons. *Oh, oh quelle horreur?* I was almost mad at this dream but it was real and I felt HE was bursting. I felt a frenzy. That's when I encountered my treasure. . . . I would have given anything to dip inside again. . . . I was electrified that your saucy crinoline let me touch your legs that only I had ever seen. . . . We fell on each other like wild cats. . . ." She is just as enthusiastic, writing: "You know I want you. I received immense pleasure and feel overwhelmed by it, pleasure incomparable to everything else," and he often replies: "compliments from mon *bingerle* which is fully armed." But they also discuss politics and war and share the happiness of their growing family of children.

When Alexander's wife died in 1880, he married Katya, now Princess Yurovskaya, but in 1881, terrorists assassinated Alexander. Katya retired to Paris. Here's one of the *bingerle* letters from early in their relationship:

> At ten in the morning.
>   Bonjour my angel, I love you more than life and am happy to love you, my heart belongs to

you totally forever. . . . I await your letter with a
feverish impatience and can't understand what
delays it.

At four in the afternoon.
    I want you more madly than ever my adored
angel. . . . The ceremony went well but I swear I am
still exhausted from our delicious *bingerles* and the
exertions of this morning, but we could once again
experience the happiness that we know together, I
would certainly not rush and never interrupt our
bingerle. Yes certainly I feel that I have become your
life and I'd only like it that you don't forget that you
are mine and I've only everywhere one idea in my
head—it's you my angel, joy, happiness, consolation,
courage, my everything. Nothing else exists for me.
Thank you for telling me that your life has become
something thanks to me. You couldn't give me a
greater pleasure because that tells me that you feel
loved and you understand what you've become for me.
Without you, my existence would be impossible and
I would follow you in into the tomb. May God pity
us and give us one day the possibility of only living
for us. There couldn't be a couple more loving. Thanks
to our delicious evening and our encounter of the
morning, I feel totally impregnated with the brilliant
and joyous moments that come to me without ceasing.
I see myself in my imagination lying in the arms of
my adorable pixie and adoring your [illegible word]
that I adore like all the rest of your darling being and
I can't forget the expression in your adorable eyes
during our *bingerles* which reflects the pleasure that

you give and that you share with the very being, body
and soul, more than ever. How can I not be mad for
you after that, my angel, my everything? So tomorrow
we have the chance to see each other in the morning
during my promenade and the evening at the wedding
where our looks will express what we feel. Monday
morning you tell what you can do and in the evening
I hope to meet to complete our interrupted
bingerle. . . . I want you to know that you delight
my being, which belongs to you for ever, it's love for
you more than ever. I would like to eat you, kiss you
taste you. . . .

Josef Stalin to Pelageya Onufrieva, 29 February 1912

The pleasure of private letters is that they sometimes reveal lost
aspects of familiar characters. Here in 1912, Josef Djugashvili, a
Bolshevik revolutionary of Georgian origins who later adopts
the name "Stalin," writes a love letter of passionate "kiiissssing"
to his schoolgirl mistress Pelageya. They have met in Vologda
where Stalin is in exile and she is the mistress of one of Stalin's friends. She is around sixteen; he is thirty-four. He lec-
tures her about Shakespeare, art, and philosophy. He calls her
"Hot Polya," and she calls him "Oddball Osip"—a diminutive
for Josef. She knows that when he leaves they would never
meet again. As the future tyrant of the Soviet Union catches
a late train to Moscow, to vanish again and return to his
work in the revolutionary underworld, he buys a postcard of
Rodin's sculpture *The Kiss*—a couple kissing—and sends this to
Polya.

Dear PG,

I got your letter today. . . . Don't write to the old address since none of us are there any more. . . . I owe you a kiss for the kiss, passed on to me by Peter. Let me kiss you now. I'm not simply sending a kiss but am kiiissssing you passionately (it's not worth kissing any other way),

Josef

Family

Elizabeth I to Mary I, 16 March 1554

This is the letter that saves a princess. It is the reign of Queen Mary, daughter of Henry VIII and Queen Catherine of Aragon—a dangerous time for her semilegitimate half sister Elizabeth, daughter of Henry VIII and his short lived queen Anne Boleyn, executed as an adulteress and regarded by Mary as a whorish Protestant heretic.

In 1553, when Henry's successor Edward VI died young, powerful factions tried to impose a Protestant monarch with a tenuous claim: Lady Jane Grey. But Mary was a king's daughter, even if she was a Catholic one, and she was accepted as rightful queen. Once she started to reimpose Catholicism and agreed to marry the Catholic King Philip of Spain, she faced a rebellion led by Thomas Wyatt, who planned to replace her with Elizabeth. To force him to implicate Elizabeth, Wyatt was tortured. He was then executed.

Elizabeth is arrested, but the intelligent and vigilant twenty-one-year-old shrewdly appeals directly to her sister. As she is about to be transferred to the sinister and looming Tower of London, where princes and princesses of royal blood have been executed or murdered, she writes this letter. She cites the recent case of the duke of Somerset, Lord Protector under the young Edward VI, who allowed the execution of his own

brother Lord Admiral Thomas Seymour for conspiracy—
and for trying to marry Elizabeth herself. It is known as
the "Tide Letter" because Elizabeth deliberately writes it so
slowly that the tide has turned before it is finished, delaying
her remand to the Tower for a day. In its well-chosen words,
we can hear one of Henry VIII's daughters begging for her
life from another. Elizabeth was later taken to the Tower, but
then released. On Mary's death, she succeeded to the throne,
becoming perhaps England's greatest monarch. Her survival
would confirm the independent and Protestant path of English
history.

> If any ever did try this old saying, "that a king's
> word was more than another man's oath," I most
> humbly beseech your Majesty to verify it to me, and
> to remember your last promise and my last demand,
> that I be not condemned without answer and due
> proof, which it seems that I now am; for without cause
> proved, I am by your council from you commanded to
> go to the Tower, a place more wanted for a false traitor
> than a true subject, which though I know I desire it
> not, yet in the face of all this realm it appears proved.
> I pray to God I may die the shamefullest death that
> any ever died, if I may mean any such thing; and to
> this present hour I protest before God (Who shall
> judge my truth, whatsoever malice shall devise), that I
> never practiced, counselled, nor consented to anything
> that might be prejudicial to your person anyway, or
> dangerous to the state by any means. And therefore
> I humbly beseech your Majesty to let me answer
> afore yourself, and not suffer me to trust to your
> Councillors, yea, and that afore I go to the Tower, if

it be possible; if not, before I be further condemned.
Howbeit, I trust assuredly your Highness will give me
leave to do it afore I go, that thus shamefully I may
not be cried out on, as I now shall be; yea, and that
without cause. Let conscience move your Highness to
pardon this my boldness, which innocency procures
me to do, together with hope of your natural kindness,
which I trust will not see me cast away without
desert, which what it is I would desire no more of
God but that you truly knew, but which thing I think
and believe you shall never by report know, unless by
yourself you hear. I have heard of many in my time
cast away for want of coming to the presence of their
Prince; and in late days I heard my Lord of Somerset
say that if his brother had been suffered to speak with
him he had never suffered; but persuasions were made
to him so great that he was brought in belief that he
could not live safely if the Admiral lived, and that
made him give consent to his death. Though these
persons are not to be compared to your Majesty,
yet I pray to God the like evil persuasions persuade
not one sister against the other, and all for that they
have heard false report, and the truth not known.
Therefore, once again, kneeling with humbleness of
heart, because I am not suffered to bow the knees of
my body, I humbly crave to speak with your Highness,
which I would not be so bold as to desire if I knew
not myself most clear, as I know myself most true.
And as for the traitor Wyatt, he might peradventure
write me a letter, but on my faith I never received any
from him. And as for the copy of the letter sent to
the French King, I pray God confound me eternally if

ever I sent him word, message, token, or letter, by any means, and to this truth I will stand in till my death.

> *Your Highness's most faithful subject, that hath been from*
> *the beginning, and will be to my end,*
> ELIZABETH

I humbly crave but only one word of answer from yourself.

Vilma Grünwald to Kurt Grünwald, 11 July 1944

Few letters survive from the death camps built by the Nazis to exterminate the Jewish people during the Holocaust. Here is an almost unreadably poignant short note, from the Czech prisoner Vilma Grünwald to her doctor husband Kurt. She, Kurt, and their two children, John and Frank (Misa), were arrested like thousands of other innocent Jewish families and transported to Auschwitz. At the selection, the SS doctor Josef Mengele sends the limping John to the left—for instant execution in the extermination camp. His mother, knowing what this means, chooses to join him in an act of maternal love. She writes this note moments after she and John have been separated from the other two, then hands it to a guard and asks him to convey it to Kurt, who would be set to work in the neighboring slave labor camp as a physician responsible for restoring injured prisoners to a state that they might work again. Vilma and John are gassed moments later.

Amazingly, the letter reached Kurt, who survived the Holocaust, and upon his release was reunited with his surviving son Frank, who eventually donated the letter to the United States Holocaust Memorial Museum.

You, my only one, dearest, in isolation we are waiting
for darkness. We considered the possibility of hiding
but decided not to do it since we felt it would be
hopeless. The famous trucks are already here and we are
waiting for it to begin. I am completely calm. You—my
only and dearest one, do not blame yourself for what
happened, it was our destiny. We did what we could.
Stay healthy and remember my words that time will
heal—if not completely—then—at least partially. Take
care of the little golden boy and don't spoil him too
much with your love. Both of you—stay healthy, my
dear ones. I will be thinking of you and Misa. Have a
fabulous life, we must board the trucks.

Into eternity, Vilma.

Kadashman-Enlil to Amenhotep III, c.1370 BC

Fathers often take a view about who their daughters should
marry, and that has not changed over the three millennia since
this letter was written. It is from one king to another, and royal
daughters have often been treated as political pawns by their
fathers.

The Babylonian king Kadashman-Enlil was a contemporary
of the Egyptian pharaoh Amenhotep III the Magnificent, and
the two were frequent correspondents.

This is one of the Amarna letters, carved on clay tablets, that
were discovered in 1887 in the new sacred capital Akhenaten
(today el-Amarna), founded by Amenhotep's son Pharaoh Akhenaten. These diplomatic letters, 382 of them, written in Akkadian
cuneiform, were probably stored in the Bureau of the Pharaoh's
Correspondence, and may well be the most revealing letters of
the early ancient world.

Here, Kadashman-Enlil smarts at the insult of being refused one of Amenhotep's daughters, before offering one of his own daughters in return for gold. Egyptian monarchs regarded themselves as far too important to give their daughters to foreign rulers—but the Babylonian is clearly irritated by this pharaonic arrogance, an irritation that may only be soothed with gold, gold, and more gold. . . .

How is it possible that, having written to you in order
to ask for the hand of your daughter—oh my brother,
you should have written me using such language,
telling me that you will not give her to me as since
earliest times no daughter of the king of Egypt has ever
been given in marriage? Why are you telling me such
things? You are the king. You may do as you wish. If
you wanted to give me your daughter in marriage who
could say you nay?
   But you, keeping to your principle of not sending
anybody, have not sent me a wife. Have you not been
looking for a fraternal and amical relationship, when
you suggested to me—in writing—a marriage, in order
to make us become closer? Why hasn't my brother sent
me a wife?
   . . . It is possible for you not to send me a wife, but
how could I refuse you a wife and not send her to you,
as you did? I have daughters, I will not refuse you in
any way concerning this. . . .
   As to the gold about which I wrote you, send
me now quickly during this summer . . . before your
messenger reaches me, gold in abundance, as much
as is available. I could thus achieve the task I have
undertaken. If you send me this summer . . . the gold

concerning which I've written to you, I shall give
you my daughter in marriage. Therefore, send gold,
willingly, as much as you please. But if you do not send
me gold . . . so I can achieve the task I have undertaken,
why haven't you sent me any earlier willingly? After I
have finished the task I have undertaken, why would
I wish for gold? Even if you sent me 3,000 talents of
gold I would not accept them. I would return them and
would not give you my daughter in marriage.

Oliver Cromwell to Valentine Walton, 4 July 1644

Even victory has its heartbreaks. Two days after his defeat of
the forces of Charles I at Marston Moor, one of the bloodiest
battles of the English Civil War and the largest ever fought
on English soil, Oliver Cromwell writes to his brother-in-
law, Valentine. He celebrates the victory as a "great favor from
the Lord" for his side, "the Godly Party," but also has to inform
Walton that his son, young Valentine, has been killed in the
battle. This is a classic letter of English history: as the Parlia-
mentarian cavalry commander, Cromwell is the military genius
who has created the Ironside cavalry that will decisively con-
tribute to victory over the king.

Born in 1599 in Huntingdon, Cromwell was an obscure
provincial gentleman until elected to Parliament at the height
of its crisis with King Charles. Having no military experience,
he recruited his own troop, ultimately commanding the New
Model Army. Ruthless and fanatically religious, known as "Old
Ironside," this psalm-singing general emerged from the Civil
War as the dominant parliamentary leader, reluctantly over-
seeing the execution of the king. In the new republic known

as the "Commonwealth" he defeated all challengers, including the Scots, and led an invasion of Ireland, during which he suppressed the Catholics in a series of massacres. In 1653 he was elected as a quasi-king with the title Lord Protector. This letter shows his sanctimony and harshness—it is hard to forget the image of mowing down the royal cavalry like "stubble to our swords" but, having lost children himself, Cromwell also shows his softer side.

To my loving Brother,
Colonel Valentine Walton: These
    It's our duty to sympathize in all mercies; and to praise the Lord together in chastisements or trials, that so we may sorrow together.
    Truly England and the Church of God hath had a great favor from the Lord, in this great victory given unto us, such as the like never was since this war began.
    It had all the evidences of an absolute victory obtained by the Lord's blessing upon the Godly Party principally. We never charged but we routed the enemy. The Left Wing, which I commanded, being our own horse, saving a few Scots in our rear, beat all the Prince's horse. God made them as stubble to our swords. We charged their regiments of foot with our horse, and routed all we charged. The particulars I cannot relate now; but I believe, of twenty thousand the Prince hath not four thousand left. Give glory, all the glory, to God.
    Sir, God hath taken away your eldest son by a cannon shot. It brake his leg. We were necessitated to have it cut off, whereof he died.
    Sir, you know my own trials this way: but the Lord

supported me with this, That the Lord took him into the happiness we all pant for and live for. There is your precious child full of glory, never to know sin or sorrow any more. He was a gallant young man, exceedingly gracious. God give you His comfort. Before his death he was so full of comfort that to Frank Russel and myself he could not express it, "It was so great above his pain." This he said to us. Indeed it was admirable. A little after, he said, One thing lay upon his spirit. I asked him, What that was? he told me it was, That God had not suffered him to be any more the executioner of His enemies. At his fall, his horse being killed with the bullet, and as I am informed three horses more, I am told he bid them, Open to the right and left, that he might see the rogues run. Truly he was exceedingly beloved in the Army, of all that knew him. But few knew him; for he was a precious young man, fit for God. You have cause to bless the Lord. He is a glorious Saint in Heaven; wherein you ought exceedingly to rejoice. Let this drink up your sorrow; seeing these are not feigned words to comfort you, but the thing is real and undoubted a truth. You may do all things by the strength of Christ. Seek that, and you shall easily bear your trial. Let this public mercy to the Church of God make you to forget your private sorrow. The Lord be your strength: so prays

Your truly faithful and loving brother,
OLIVER CROMWELL

Toussaint L'Ouverture to Napoleon, 12 July 1802

"I was born a slave but nature gave me the soul of a free man." François-Dominique Toussaint was a black slave on the French colony Sainte-Domingue on the island of Hispaniola. Intelligent, gifted, and educated, he was freed from slavery and then managed a French plantation as well as somehow picking up a mix of Western and Creole medical knowledge, ultimately running his own estate with his own slaves. But in 1791, the French Revolution inspired a rebellion by the slaves of the island and he soon emerged as their leader. By 1793, he had earned the nickname L'Ouverture, "The Opener," in battle, and made this declaration: "Brothers and friends, I am Toussaint L'Ouverture; perhaps my name has made itself known to you. I have undertaken vengeance. I want Liberty and Equality to reign in St. Domingue. I am working to make that happen. Unite yourselves to us, brothers, and fight with us for the same cause."

Fighting first with the Spanish against the French, then vice versa, then against the French again, L'Ouverture became governor-general, autocrat for life of the first black republic, issuing a constitution while remaining formally under France. Napoleon Bonaparte, first consul of France, sent an army. L'Ouverture ordered his commander Dessalines to burn Port-au-Prince: "Set that place on fire. . . . Don't forget we have no other resource than destruction and flames. . . . Tear up the roads with shot; throw corpses and horses into all the fountains; burn and annihilate everything in order that those who've come to reduce us to slavery may before their eyes have the image of hell they deserve." But Toussaint was tricked and captured. His wife, Suzanne, and family were arrested. Here, held on a French warship, the broken Toussaint writes this pitiful letter begging for the freedom of his family. Shipped to France, he died in prison but within a year, the French were defeated and his creation, Haiti, achieved independence.

CITIZEN FIRST CONSUL: I will not conceal my faults from you. I have committed some. What man is exempt? I am quite ready to avow them. After the word of honour of the Captain-General who represents the French Government, after a proclamation addressed to the colony, in which he promised to throw the veil of oblivion over the events which had taken place in Saint Domingo, I, as you did on the 18th Brumaire, withdrew into the bosom of my family. Scarcely had a month passed away, when evil-disposed persons, by means of intrigues, effected my ruin with the General-in-chief, by filling his mind with distrust against me. I received a letter from him which ordered me to act in conjunction with General Brunet. I obeyed. Accompanied by two persons, I went to Gonaïves, where I was arrested. They sent me on board the frigate Creole, I know not for what reason, without any other clothes than those I had on. The next day my house was exposed to pillage; my wife and my children were arrested; they had nothing, not even the means to cover themselves.

Citizen First Consul: A mother fifty years of age may deserve the indulgence and the kindness of a generous and liberal nation. She has no account to render. I alone ought to be responsible for my conduct to the Government I have served. I have too high an idea of the greatness and the justice of the First Magistrate of the French people, to doubt a moment of its impartiality. I indulge the feeling that the balance in its

hands will not incline to one side more than to another.
I claim its generosity.

Salutations and respect,
Toussaint Louverture

Alexander I to his sister Catherine,
20 September 1805

This letter shows how royal families are different from the rest
of us. Tsar Alexander I was tall, blonde, handsome, and all-
powerful, but he was also flawed: he colluded in the murder of
his own father, a crime he never recovered from. His greatest
love was "Catiche," the little sister who was so much younger
that he treated her more like a girlfriend than a sibling. In 1805,
as Alexander confronts Napoleon for the first time, he writes
her what amount to half love letters, saying he wants to kiss
the nose and feet of "the Little Mad Thing." But in some ways,
Catiche was tougher than Alexander. A few weeks after this, he
was catastrophically defeated by Napoleon.

Absurd Little Mad Thing,
     Get out of your head that to answer you is a trouble
to me. As soon as I have a moment it is a real pleasure,
for I love few things in the world like my Bisiam.
     The news you gave me of Aunt was a real pleasure
to me, if she is kind enough to think of me. I assure
you no day goes by without my thinking of her. Tell
her so, I beg of you, from me. Farewell, light of my
eyes, adored of my heart, polestar of the age, wonder of
Nature, or better than all these, Bisiam Bisiamovna with
the snub nose.

There is a lot left of the white grease which they put
on the wheels. I should like to send you some to keep
up that kind of softness in the muscles of the nose on
which I press the tenderest of kisses.

All yours, heart and soul, Alexander.

Charles I to Charles II, 29 November 1648

Charles I succeeded his father, James I, in 1625. Determined to
rule without the restraints of an overmighty Parliament, Charles
was successful in this respect until multiple crises forced him to
call a new Parliament in 1640. The confrontation between king
and Parliament, exacerbated by religious conflicts, led to a civil
war that Charles ultimately lost. Here, in late 1648, as Oliver
Cromwell and his New Model Army consolidate control of the
kingdom, Charles I is being held by parliamentary forces in
Newport where, after a failed attempt to escape to the continent, he is engaged in fruitless negotiations to save both his
throne and life.

Charles knows that many on the parliamentary side now
regard him as a feckless "Man of Blood" who can no longer be
trusted, and support a republic. Even the unthinkable is now
possible: the trial and execution of a divinely sanctioned monarch. Most of the royal family, including his beloved wife Hen-
rietta Maria, have escaped to the continent. Their eldest son
Charles, prince of Wales, is in the Hague. The king writes to
his son, knowing he may never see him again. It is a letter on
kingship—but also on how to behave and how to live—from a
doomed father to a faraway son.

In January 1649 the king was tried, sentenced to death, and
beheaded. England became a republic and protectorate until
1660, when the son acceded to the throne as Charles II.

NEWPORT, NOVEMBER 29, 1648

Son,

By what hath been said, you may see how long
we have labored in search of peace. Do not you be
discouraged to tread these ways, to restore yourself
to your right; but prefer the way of peace. Show the
greatness of your mind, rather to conquer your enemies
by pardoning than punishing. If you saw how unmanly
and unchristianly this implacable disposition is in our
evil willers, you would avoid that spirit. Censure us
not, for having parted with too much of our own right;
the price was great; the commodity was security to
us, peace to our people. And we are confident another
Parliament would remember how useful a King's power
is to a people's liberty.

Of how much have we divested ourself, that we
and they might meet again in a due Parliamentary
way to agree the bounds for Prince and people! And
in this, give belief to our experience, never to affect
more greatness or prerogative than what is really and
intrinsically for the good of our subjects (not satisfaction
of favorites). And if you thus use it, you will never want
means to be a father to all, and a bountiful Prince to
any you would be extraordinarily gracious to. You may
perceive all men trust their treasure, where it returns
them interest: and if Princes, like the sea, receive and
repay all the fresh streams and rivers trust them with,
they will not grudge, but pride themselves, to make
them up an ocean.

These considerations may make you a great Prince,
as your father is now a low one; and your state may be so
much the more established, as mine hath been shaken.

For subjects have learned (we dare say) that victories over their Princes are but triumphs over themselves; and so, will be more unwilling to hearken to changes hereafter.

The English nation are a sober people; however at present under some infatuation. We know not but this may be the last time we may speak to you or the world publicly. We are sensible into what hands we are fallen; and yet we bless God we have those inward refreshments, that the malice of our enemies cannot disturb. We have learned to own ourself by retiring into ourself, and therefore can the better digest what befalls us; not doubting but God can restrain our enemies' malice, and turn their fierceness unto his praise.

To conclude, if God give you success, use it humbly and far from revenge. If He restore you to your right upon hard conditions, whatever you promise, keep. Those men which have forced laws which they were bound to observe, will find their triumphs full of troubles. Do not think anything in this world worth obtaining by foul and unjust means.

You are the son of our love; and, as we direct you to what we have recommended to you, so we assure you, we do not more affectionately pray for you (to whom we are a natural parent) than we do, that the ancient glory and renown of this nation be not buried in irreligion and fanatic humor: and that all our subjects (to whom we are a political parent) may have such sober thoughts as to seek their peace in the orthodox profession of the Christian religion, as it was established since the Reformation in this kingdom, and not in new revelation; and that the ancient laws, with the interpretation according to the known practices, may once again be a hedge about them; that you may in due time govern, and they be governed, as in the fear of the Lord.

C.R

Svetlana Stalina to her father, Josef Stalin, mid-1930s

What happens when your children decide to play dictator for a day? Growing up in the Kremlin, Svetlana, the daughter of the Soviet dictator Josef Stalin, likes to play this game. From the age of seven to eleven, she often writes orders that every child in the world would love to put into effect. One day, she orders her "First Secretary" (Stalin) and other "Secretaries" (of the Communist Party) that all homework be cancelled in all Soviet schools. Stalin enormously enjoyed playing the game and signed all her orders, as did the rest of the politburo. They were then pinned up on the board in the Stalin kitchen. Stalin called her "Svetlana the Boss" or "Setanka, Mistress of the House," and usually answered: "I obey. Setanka's little secretary. Stalin." Svetlana signed herself "First Secretary of the Communist Party" or "Boss." In this "order," she demands to know what is really happening in the very secretive ruling Central Committee through which her father terrorized the Soviet people. Sometimes Stalin requested more orders: "write to me more often: your Little Secretary [Stalin] will soon not know what to do if he doesn't receive your daily orders and commands."

Daily Order No. 3. I order you to show me what happens in the Central Committee! Strictly confidential. Stalina, the Boss.

Augustus to Caius Caesar, 23 September AD 2

An elderly father writes to his son; an aging emperor writes to his adopted heir. Caesar Augustus (formerly Octavian) has ruled Rome since the assassination of his great-uncle Julius Caesar in 44 BC and the entire empire as its first emperor since 31. Having no sons of his own, he has adopted his nephews Caius and Lucius to succeed him at his "sentry post." Sending Caius on an inspection trip of the Roman provinces, he finds that on his sixty-fourth birthday he is missing the "dearest little donkey." Sadly, both boys were to die before Augustus himself.

> Greetings my dear Caius my dearest little donkey whom, so help me, I constantly miss whenever you are away from me. But especially on such days as today my eyes are eager for my Caius and wherever you have been today I hope you have celebrated my sixty-fourth birthday in health and happiness . . . and I pray the gods that whatever time is left for me I may pass with you safe and well with our country in a flourishing condition while you both are playing the man and preparing to succeed to my sentry post.

Joseph II to his brother Leopold II, 4 October 1777

It was the royal wedding of its time—but seven years into the marriage, something is wrong, and this letter reveals what that is and how to solve it.

In 1770, when she was just fifteen, the Habsburg archduchess of Austria, Marie Antoinette married the Bourbon heir to the French throne, soon to be Louis XVI. She was pretty and playful but also silly, extravagant, and unwise. This promised to be a bad combination in an overstretched kingdom on the verge of bankruptcy, which could ill afford any loss of royal prestige. King Louis, for his part, was cloddish, ineffectual, and dull. For seven years, while Marie flirted with admirers, Louis struggled to consummate the marriage.

Finally her brother, Emperor Joseph II, comes to visit to see if he can help. In an early example of marriage counselling, Joseph interviews Louis and his sister like an imperial sex therapist. "What a pair of blunderers," he writes afterward in this astonishing letter to his brother, the future Emperor Leopold, concluding that the real problem is not a physical or medical one but merely the queen's lack of interest and the king's laziness. In August the grateful couple consummated their marriage, and she was soon pregnant with the first of several children. In 1789 Louis and Marie Antoinette were overthrown and, in 1793, guillotined.

> Imagine! In his marriage bed—this is the secret— he has strong, perfectly satisfactory erections. He introduces the member, stays there for perhaps two minutes without moving, withdraws without ever discharging but still erect, and bids good night. It's incredible, because in addition he sometimes has nighttime emissions, but in his bed, never when on the job, and he's happy, saying simply that he only does it out of duty and gets no pleasure from it. Ah! If I could have been present once, I should have arranged it properly. He needs to be whipped, to make him discharge in a passion, like donkeys. Further, my sister is pretty placid, and they're two incompetents together.

Rameses the Great to Ḫattušili III, 1243 BC

The arrogance of empire in a letter three thousand years old. Rameses the Great ruled Egypt at its zenith, its master for around fifty years. Earlier in his reign he had fought against the Hittite king Ḫattušili, but in 1258 BC, following the Battle of Kadesh, they became allies and Rameses deigned to marry a Hittite princess. Here, taking advantage of their good relations, Ḫattušili asks Rameses if he can help with a sensitive family problem: his sister Matanazi, married to a nearby king, wants to have children even though she is no longer young, and the Hittite asks if Rameses can send priests and healers to make this happen. Here is the Great King's patronizing and ungracious answer, sneering that not even Egyptian magic could make a woman of sixty produce children. . . .

Thus to my Brother: (Concerning) what my Brother has written to me regarding his sister Matanazi: "May my Brother send to me a man to prepare medicines so that she may bear children." So has my Brother written. And so (I say) to my Brother: "Look, Matanazi, the sister of my Brother, the king your Brother knows her. She is said to be 50 or even 60 years old! Look, a woman of 50 is old, to say nothing of a 60-year-old! One can't produce medicines to enable her to bear children! Well, the Sun God and the Storm God may give a command, and the order which they give will then be carried out continually for the sister of my Brother. And I, the king your Brother, will send an expert incantation-priest and an expert doctor and they will prepare medicines to assist her to produce children.

Creation

Michelangelo to Giovanni da Pistoia, 1509

Michelangelo Buonarroti was not only a sculptor and artist but also a brilliant poet and a superb letter writer. Sometimes he sent his poems as letters—this is one of the best. He had been hired by the warrior-pope Julius II in 1508 to supervise the painting of the ceiling of the Sistine Chapel in Rome: a somewhat unorthodox choice, given that he was better known as a sculptor at the time.

Julius let Michelangelo "do as I liked"—nine main scenes that would represent God's creation of the world and of man in Genesis. The work, which would take him until 1512, would be his most timeless achievement. Not only was his vision astonishingly ambitious, but the physical strain of actually painting the ceiling was punishing. He had to build his own scaffolding and hang upside down high above the chapel for hours on end, year after year. At one point he writes to his father: "I lead a miserable existence . . . not of life nor honor. . . . I live wearied by stupendous labors and beset by a thousand anxieties . . . never an hour's happiness have I had." Out of these agonies emerges one of the greatest works of art in the human story. A year into the work's creation, he sends this despairing verse letter to his friend Giovanni da Pistoia, detailing some of the torments that he faced.

"When the Author was Painting the Vault of the Sistine Chapel"

I've already grown a goiter from this torture,
swollen up here like a cat from Lombardy
(or anywhere where the stagnant water's poison).
My stomach's squashed under my chin, my beard's
pointing at heaven, my brain's crushed in a casket,
my breast twists like a harpy's. My brush,
above me all the time, dribbles the paint
so my face makes a fine floor for droppings!
My haunches are grinding into my guts,
my poor ass strains to work as a counterweight,
every gesture I make is blind and aimless.
My skin hangs loose below me, my spine's
all knotted from folding over itself,
I'm bent taut as a Syrian bow.

And because I'm like this, my thoughts
Are crazy perfidious tripe:
Anyone shoots badly through a crooked blowpipe.

My painting is dead.
Defend it for me, Giovanni, protect my honor.
I am not in the right place—I am not a painter.

Wolfgang Amadeus Mozart to his cousin Marianne,
13 November 1777

A letter of manic and scatological exuberance from a musical genius. Brought up in Salzburg and taught music by his ambitious choirmaster father, the young Mozart toured Europe for ten years as a performing pianist and violinist. During the stress of endless touring when he was in his twenties, Mozart enjoyed a madcap friendship and probably passionate relationship with Marianne—much to his father's disapproval. Their sexual collusion and relish in fecal humor is only too clear in their earthily hilarious letters: "I shall greet you high and nobly with pizzazz," writes Mozart to the little cousin he called "Basle," "and put my personal seal on your ass, I will kiss your hands and have such fun shooting off my rear-end gun, I shall embrace you with a smack and wash you down front and back, I shall pay all I owed you from the start and then let go a resounding fart and perhaps even drop something hard—well adieu my Angel my heart I'm waiting for you PS Shit-dibitare, shit-dibatate, the pastor of Rodempl, he licked the ass of his kitchen maid, to set a good example."

The child prodigy was first employed by the prince-bishop of Salzburg. Then in 1781, determined to make his name, he arrived in Vienna. He thrived creatively in the musical capital of Europe, where he composed his greatest operas and symphonies. But he was only moderately appreciated by Emperor Joseph II, who finally appointed him to the rank of chamber composer. In 1782 Mozart married Constance Weber, whom he adored: they had six children. His letters to her are boyishly affectionate: "I get all excited like a child when I think about being with you again—If people could see into my heart I should almost feel ashamed. Everything is cold to me— ice-cold.—If you were here with me, maybe I would find the courtesies people are showing me more enjoyable—but as it is, it's all so empty—adieu—my dear—I am Forever, your Mozart who loves you with his entire soul. PS.—while I was writing the last page, tear after tear fell on the paper. But I must cheer up—

catch—An astonishing number of kisses are flying about—
The deuce!—I see a whole crowd of them. Ha! Ha! I have just
caught three—They are delicious. . . . I kiss you millions of
times."

But nothing quite approaches the outrageous humor of the
"Basle letters," those earlier Mozartian creations, with their
anarchic stream of puns, alliteration, songs, echoes, and rep-
etitions. They are best read very fast. This one begins with an
instruction from his mother to write a "sensible letter." But that
resolution did not last long. . . .

> . . . now write her a sensible letter for once, you can still
> write all that funny stuff, but be sure to tell her that you
> have received all the mail, so she won't be concerned
> about it, and worry.
>
> Ma très chère Nièce! Cousine! fille!
> 　　Mère, Sœur, et Épouse!
>
> Heaven, Hell, and a thousand sacristies, Croatians,
> damnations, devils, and witchies, druids, cross-
> Battalions with no ends, by all the elements, air, water,
> earth, and fire, Europe, asia, affrica, and America,
> jesuits, Augustins, Benedictins, Capucins, Minorites,
> Franciscans, Dominicans, Carthusians, and dignified
> Holy-Crucians, Canons regular and irregular, and all
> hairy brutes and snitches, higgledy-piggledy castrates
> and bitches, asses, buffaloes, oxen, fools, nitwits, and
> fops! What sort of manner is this, my dear? 4 soldiers
> and only 3 gear?—such a Paquet no Portrait?—I was
> already filled with high expectations—I thought for
> sure—for you wrote it to me yourself not long ago that
> I would receive it soon, very soon. Are you perhaps

doubting whether I will keep my word?—I certainly hope that you have no doubts! Well then, I beg you, do send it to me, the sooner, the better. And I hope it will portray you the way I requested, I mean in french fashion.

How I like Mannheim?—as well as one can like any place without Bäasle. Pardon my poor handwriting, the pen is already old; now I have been shitting for nearly 22 years out of the same old hole and yet it's not torn a whit!—although I used it so often to shit—and then chewed off the muck bit by bit.

I hope, on the other hand, that you have been receiving my letters, as it so happens, one from Hohenaltheim, 2 from Mannheim, and now this one. As it so happens, this one is the third from Mannheim, but all in all it's the 4th, as it so happens. Now I must close, as it so happens, because I am not dressed yet, and we'll be eating soon so that afterward we can go and shit again, as it so happens. Do go on loving me as I love you, then we'll stop loving each other. . . . [in French] Farewell, I hope that you would already have taken some French lessons, and I wouldn't doubt that— Listen: you would know better French than I because I certainly haven't written a word in this language in two years. Farewell. I kiss your hands, your face, your knees and your—at any rate, all that you permit me to kiss.

I am with all my heart
your
very affectionate Nephew and Cousin
Wolfg. Amadé Mozart

Honoré de Balzac to Ewelina Hánska, 19 June 1836

Here is the power of the letter. Balzac, author of the Comédie Humaine novels, begins his relationship with the Polish countess Hánska without them ever having met. Daughter of a famous and rich aristocratic family, she married a landowner twenty-four years older than her and had five children by him. During the 1820s, she started to read Balzac's novels and, in 1832, sent an anonymous letter from Poland to Paris. She is a fan and a married woman; he, a flattered and vain celebrity. After about a year they meet and begin their affair. Although Hánska's husband discovers their letters, Balzac is able to convince him that they are just a game.

When the count died in 1841, Balzac might have believed that the path was clear for the two of them to marry, but ill health and financial worries meant that they did not wed until March 1850, just months before his own death in August. This letter from early in their relationship shows the near obsession that Balzac has with Hánska, though there is a hint that her love is burning up his creative juices. If the husband had read this letter, would he have believed it was just a game?

MY BELOVED ANGEL,

   I am nearly mad about you, as much as one can be mad: I cannot bring together two ideas that you do not interpose yourself between them. I can no longer think of nothing but you. In spite of myself, my imagination carries me to you. I grasp you, I kiss you, I caress you, a thousand of the most amorous caresses take possession of me. As for my heart, there you will always be—very much so. I have a delicious sense of you there. But my God, what is to become of me, if you have deprived

me of my reason? This is a monomania which, this
morning, terrifies me. I rise up every moment say to
myself, "Come, I am going there!" Then I sit down
again, moved by the sense of my obligations. There
is a frightful conflict. This is not a life. I have never
before been like that. You have devoured everything.
I feel foolish and happy as soon as I let myself think
of you. I whirl round in a delicious dream in which in
one instant I live a thousand years. What a horrible
situation! Overcome with love, feeling love in every
pore, living only for love, and seeing oneself consumed
by griefs, and caught in a thousand spiders' threads.
O, my darling Eva, you did not know it. I picked up
your card. It is there before me, and I talked to you as
if you were here. I see you, as I did yesterday, beautiful,
astonishingly beautiful. Yesterday, during the whole
evening, I said to myself "She is mine!" Ah! The angels
are not as happy in Paradise as I was yesterday!

Pablo Picasso to Marie-Thérèse Walter, 19 July 1939

An obsessional commitment to art and love is the theme of
this letter. Pablo Picasso lived for his work, and everything else
in his life was subordinate to his frenzied, mutating quest for
artistic expression, often inspired by his female muses. Olga
Khokhlova, a Russian ballerina, was his muse-lover during his
synthetic cubism period; they married, but the relationship did
not last. He was forty-six and married to Olga when he spotted
seventeen-year-old blonde Marie-Thérèse Walter in the street.
They fell in love—though he remained married. Living between
Paris and a rented French country house, he painted her many
times, and she became the muse for some of his most joyous

masterpieces such as *Girl before a Mirror, Le Rêve,* and *Nude in a Black Armchair.* It was a period of intense creativity that reached a climax in the year 1932 at the Château de Boisgeloup in Normandy.

In bursts of color, Marie-Thérèse appears blonde and sensuous. In 1935 she gives birth to their daughter Maya. This letter reflects in rhapsodic tones his almost carnivorous, all-consuming love for his young mistress. The "problems in Switzerland" he refers to are probably business issues occasioned by the imminent outbreak of the Second World War.

But the artist was already focusing on his next muse, Dora Maar. Walter was highly jealous of the artist's new mistress: when the two girls met at his studio and demanded he choose one of them, he told them to fight it out—"one of my choicest moments." Marie-Thérèse lived on in Paris and survived the artist. Nine years after his death in 1973, she committed suicide.

My love,

I have just received your letter. I wrote several to you which you must have received by now. I love you more each day. You are everything to me. I will sacrifice everything for you, for our everlasting love. I Love you. I could never forget you my love and if I am unhappy it is because I don't belong to you as I would have liked. My Love, my Love, my Love, but I want for you to be happy and to think only of being happy. I would give anything for that. I am having some problems in Switzerland—but all that is not important. Let them send all the tears to me if I can prevent you from shedding one. I love you. Kiss Maya our daughter and I embrace you a thousand thousand times.

Yours, Picasso.

John Keats to Fanny Brawne, 13 October 1819

Here is the ultimate celebration of all-consuming passion and doom-laden romanticism. John Keats, born in 1795, was cursed with ill health, poverty, and a desperation worthy of the outstanding Romantic poet. His mother died of tuberculosis when he was fourteen, and he felt surrounded by death on all sides.

In 1818 he meets Fanny Brawne, who becomes the love of his life, but he is too poor to get engaged to her and their love is never consummated. His agonizing obsessions with Fanny, love, and death inspired the poems "The Eve of St. Agnes" and "La Belle Dame sans Merci"—also expressed in this letter to Fanny. Soon afterward, Keats discovered that he too had tuberculosis and moved to Rome for his health, where he perished at the age of just twenty-six.

Fanny mourned him for six years, sharing her devotion with the poet's sister Fanny Keats. Finally Brawne got married to a Jewish merchant's son named Louis Lindon with whom she had a family. Just before her death in 1865, she revealed her relationship with Keats to her children and gave them his letters to her, which would "someday be considered of value." The children published the letters, leading many to accuse Fanny of being unworthy of the poet. It was the much-later publication of her letters to Keats's sister that proved how she had cherished Keats's exquisite art.

25 COLLEGE STREET, WESTMINSTER

My dearest Girl,

This moment I have set myself to copy some verses out fair. I cannot proceed with any degree of content. I must write you a line or two and see if that will assist in

dismissing you from my Mind for ever so short
a time. Upon my Soul I can think of nothing else—
The time is passed when I had power to advise and
warn you against the unpromising morning of my
Life—My love has made me selfish. I cannot exist
without you—I am forgetful of everything but seeing
you again—my Life seems to stop there—I see no
further. You have absorb'd me. I have a sensation
at the present moment as though I was dissolving—
I should be exquisitely miserable without the hope of
soon seeing you. I should be afraid to separate myself
far from you. My sweet Fanny, will your heart never
change? My love, will it? I have no limit now to my
love—Your note came in just here—I cannot be happier
away from you—'T is richer than an Argosy of Pearles.
Do not threat me even in jest. I have been astonished
that Men could die Martyrs for religion—I have
shudder'd at it—I shudder no more. I could be martyr'd
for my Religion—Love is my religion—I could die
for that—I could die for you. My Creed is Love and
you are its only tenet—You have ravish'd me away by
a Power I cannot resist; and yet I could resist till I saw
you; and even since I have seen you I have endeavored
often "to reason against the reasons of my Love." I can
do that no more—the pain would be too great—My
Love is selfish. I cannot breathe without you.

Yours for ever
John Keats

T. S. Eliot to George Orwell, 13 July 1944

Every writer dreads a rejection slip from a publisher. Here the publisher of Faber and Faber, who happens to be T. S. Eliot—better known as the poet of *The Waste Land*—pompously rejects the latest book by George Orwell, journalist, essayist, and novelist. Orwell was best known at the time for having fought in the Spanish Civil War and for his brilliant work of reportage covering it, published as *Homage to Catalonia,* as well as for books on his personal experiences of poverty like *The Road to Wigan Pier.* But now he is doing something dangerous for any writer: changing his genre. In his latest work, he has used the metaphor of a farmyard to show how Soviet Russia—or a tyranny like it—becomes a murderous terror state. It is clearly an attack on Stalinism at a time when Stalin's Russia was an ally in the war against Hitler. Orwell was more sympathetic to Stalin's rival, Trotsky. Hence Eliot's point—missing the much wider message of the novel. *Animal Farm,* followed by his novel *1984,* were masterpieces that observed and warned against the Orwellian realities of modern politics that remain utterly relevant in the twenty-first century. Eliot's patronizing rejection must rank as one of the most embarrassing mistakes in publishing history.

Dear Orwell

I know that you wanted a quick decision about "Animal Farm": but the minimum is two directors' opinions, and that can't be done under a week. But for the importance of speed, I should have asked the Chairman to look at it as well. But the other director is in agreement with me on the main points. We agree that it is a distinguished piece of writing; that the fable is very skilfully handled, and that the narrative keeps one's interest on its own plane—and that is something very few authors have achieved since Gulliver.

On the other hand, we have no conviction (and I am sure none of the other directors would have) that this is the right point of view from which to criticize the political situation at the present time. It is certainly the duty of any publishing firm which pretends to other interests and motives than mere commercial prosperity, to publish books which go against the current of the moment: but in each instance that demands that at least one member of the firm should have the conviction that this is the thing that needs saying at the moment. I can't see any reason of prudence or caution to prevent anybody from publishing this book—if he believed in what it stands for.

Now I think my own dissatisfaction with this apologue is that the effect is simply one of negation. It ought to excite some sympathy with what the author wants, as well as sympathy with his objections to something: and the positive point of view, which I take to be generally Trotskyite, is not convincing. I think you split your vote, without getting any compensating stronger adhesion from either party—i.e. those who criticize Russian tendencies from the point of view of a purer communism, and those who, from a very different point of view, are alarmed about the future of small nations. And after all, your pigs are far more intelligent than the other animals, and therefore the best qualified to run the farm—in fact, there couldn't have been an Animal Farm at all without them: so that what was needed, (someone might argue), was not more communism but more public-spirited pigs.

I am very sorry, because whoever publishes this, will naturally have the opportunity of publishing your future work: and I have a regard for your work, because it is good writing of fundamental integrity.

Miss Sheldon will be sending you the script under separate cover.

Courage

Sarah Bernhardt to Mrs. Patrick Campbell, 1915

She was the most famous actress of the late nineteenth and early twentieth centuries who could teach a lot to the celebrities of today. The beautiful daughter of a Parisian Jewish courtesan and an unknown client, Sarah Bernhardt was a self-made woman. One of her mother's lovers was Emperor Napoleon III's powerful half brother the Duc de Morny, who helped her and may also have been the daughter's lover, too. Sarah was a free spirit as well as a brilliant thespian. When she had her only son, she refused to name the father, sometimes joking "I could never make up my mind whether his father was [Premier] Gambetta, [novelist] Victor Hugo, or General Boulanger," though he was also possibly the son of her first love the Prince de Ligne. Either way, she became France's top actress, rich and grand, constantly touring—as this letter shows. When she fell fifteen feet from a balcony during a performance of *La Tosca* in Rio de Janeiro, she broke her knee. She tolerated the agony for years until, as she laconically confides here to another famous actress "Mrs. Pat," she decides aged seventy to do something about it once and for all. . . .

Doctor will cut off my leg next Monday. Am very happy. Kisses all my heart.

Sarah Bernhardt.

Fanny Burney to her sister Esther, 22 March 1812

Frances "Fanny" Burney, born in 1752, was the daughter of a
highly cultured father—a composer and writer—and a French
mother. In a long and eventful life, her literary gifts, her curiosity and sense of humor make her a groundbreaking woman
in a man's world. Fanny started to write at a very young age,
and she became one of the first bestselling female novelists
at a time when well-born girls were not expected to dabble
in disreputable storytelling. For this reason, she published
her first novel *Evelina* anonymously, even trying to conceal her
female identity from the publisher. The witty satire on aristocratic society was a success and she became famous when
her identity was revealed. While keeping a remarkable diary
of personal and historical events from the age of sixteen to her
death in 1840 and of course writing superb letters, Fanny went
on to write a series of novels that helped inspire later writers
like Jane Austen—her novel *Cecilia* was the source of the title
of Austen's best-known novel: "The whole of this unfortunate
business," says one of Fanny's characters, "has been the result
of pride and prejudice."

Fanny had romances with various suitors but remained
unmarried for a long time, turning down unappetising marriage
proposals because she had "no idea why the single life should
not be happy. Liberty is not without its value—with woman as
well as with men." In 1785, Queen Charlotte, George III's wife,
offered her the job of Keeper of the Robes and she became a
courtier for five stressful years. She sympathized with the mod-
erate ideas of the French Revolution, finally marrying exiled
general Alexandre d'Arblay, who returned to his homeland to
serve Napoleon. While living in Paris, Fanny noticed a lump in

her breast—and agreed to undergo a mastectomy, performed
by Dr. Dubois, the accoucheur of Napoleon's empress Marie-
Louise, in the manner of a battlefield operation. Amazingly
she survived and lived on for almost thirty years. She describes
every second of the agony in this unforgettable letter to her
sister.

ACCOUNT FROM PARIS
OF A TERRIBLE
OPERATION—1812

I have promised my dearest Esther a Volume—&
here it is: I am at this moment quite well. . . . Read,
therefore, this narrative at your leisure, & without
emotion—for all has ended happily. . . .

   About August, in the year 1810, I began to be
annoyed by a small pain in my breast, which went
on augmenting from week to week, yet, being rather
heavy than acute, without causing me any uneasiness
with respect to consequences. . . . Thus passed some
months, during which Madame de Maisonneuve, my
particularly intimate friend, joined with M. d'Arblay
to press me to consent to an examination. I thought
their fears groundless, and could not make so great
a conquest over my repugnance. I relate this false
confidence, now, as a warning to my dear Esther. . . .
M. d'A summoned a physician . . . he gave me some
directions that produced no fruit—on the contrary, I
grew worse, & M. d'A now would take no denial to my
consulting M. Dubois, who had already attended &
cured me in an abscess of which Maria, my dearest
Esther, can give you the history. M. Dubois, the most

celebrated surgeon of France, was then appointed
accoucheur to the Empress. . . . I began to perceive my
real danger, M. Dubois gave me a prescription to be
pursued for a month, during which time he could not
undertake to see me again, & pronounced nothing—
but uttered so many charges to me to be tranquil, &
to suffer no uneasiness, that I could not but suspect
there was room for terrible inquietude. . . . I took, but
vainly, my prescription, & every symptom grew more
serious. . . .

A formal consultation now was held, of [doctors]
Larrey, Ribe, & Moreau—and, in time, I was formally
condemned to an operation by all Three. I was as
much astonished as disappointed—for the poor breast
was no where discolored, & not much larger than
its healthy neighbor. Yet I felt the evil to be deep, so
deep, that I often thought if it could not be dissolved,
it could only with life be extirpated. I called up,
however, all the reason I possessed, or could assume, &
told them that—if they saw no other alternative, I
would not resist their opinion & experience:—the
good Dr. Larrey, who, during his long attendance had
conceived for me the warmest friendship, had now
tears in his Eyes; from my dread he had expected
resistance . . .

I strolled to the Sallon [on the day of surgery]—I
saw it fitted with preparations, & I recoiled—But I
soon returned; to what effect disguise from myself
what I must so soon know?—yet the sight of the
immense quantity of bandages, compresses, sponges,
Lint—made me a little sick:—I walked backward &
forwards till I quieted all emotion, & became, by

degrees, nearly stupid—torpid, without sentiment
or consciousness;—& thus I remained till the Clock
struck three . . . my room, without previous message,
was entered by 7 Men in black, Dr. Larry, M. Dubois,
Dr. Moreau, Dr. Aumont, Dr. Ribe, & a pupil of Dr.
Larry, & another of M. Dubois. I was now awakened
from my stupor—& by a sort of indignation—Why
so many? & without leave?—But I could not utter a
syllable. M. Dubois acted as Commander in Chief. Dr.
Larry kept out of sight; M. Dubois ordered a Bed stead
into the middle of the room. Astonished, I turned to
Dr. Larry, who had promised that an Arm Chair would
suffice; but he hung his head, & would not look at me.
Two old mattrasses M. Dubois then demanded, & an
old Sheet. I now began to tremble violently, more with
distaste & horror of the preparations even than of the
pain. These arranged to his liking, he desired me to
mount the Bed stead. I stood suspended, for a moment,
whether I should not abruptly escape—I looked at the
door, the windows—I felt desperate—but it was only
for a moment, my reason then took the command, &
my fears & feelings struggled vainly against it. . . . I
knew not, positively, then, the immediate danger, but
every thing convinced me danger was hovering about
me, & that this experiment could alone save me from
its jaws. I mounted, therefore, unbidden, the Bed
stead—& M. Dubois placed me upon the mattrass, &
spread a cambric handkerchief upon my face. It was
transparent, however, & I saw, through it, that the
Bed stead was instantly surrounded by the 7 men &
my nurse. I refused to be held; but when, Bright
through the cambric, I saw the glitter of polished

Steel—I closed my Eyes. I would not trust to
convulsive fear the sight of the terrible incision. A
silence the most profound ensued, which lasted for
some minutes, during which, I imagine, they took their
orders by signs, & made their examination—Oh what
a horrible suspension!—I did not breathe. . . . I feared
they imagined the whole breast infected—feared it
too justly,—for, again through the Cambric, I saw
the hand of M. Dubois held up, while his forefinger
first described a straight line from top to bottom
of the breast, secondly a Cross, & thirdly a circle;
intimating that the Whole was to be taken off. . . . I
closed once more my Eyes, relinquishing all watching,
all resistance, all interference, & sadly resolute to be
wholly resigned.

My dearest Esther,—& all my dears to whom
she communicates this doleful ditty, will rejoice
to hear that this resolution once taken, was firmly
adhered to, in defiance of a terror that surpasses all
description, & the most torturing pain. Yet—when the
dreadful steel was plunged into the breast—cutting
through veins—arteries—flesh—nerves—I needed
no injunctions not to restrain my cries. I began a
scream that lasted unintermittingly during the whole
time of the incision—& I almost marvel that it rings
not in my Ears still! so excruciating was the agony.
When the wound was made, & the instrument was
withdrawn, the pain seemed undiminished, for the air
that suddenly rushed into those delicate parts felt like
a mass of minute but sharp & forked poniards, that
were tearing the edges of the wound—but when again
I felt the instrument—describing a curve—cutting
against the grain, if I may so say, while the flesh

resisted in a manner so forcible as to oppose & tire
the hand of the operator, who was forced to change
from the right to the left—then, indeed, I thought I
must have expired. I attempted no more to open my
Eyes,—they felt as if hermetically shut, & so firmly
closed, that the Eyelids seemed indented into the
Cheeks. The instrument this second time withdrawn,
I concluded the operation over—Oh no! presently the
terrible cutting was renewed—& worse than ever, to
separate the bottom, the foundation of this dreadful
gland from the parts to which it adhered—Again all
description would be baffled—yet again all was not
over,—Dr. Larry rested but his own hand, &—Oh
Heaven!—I then felt the Knife rackling against the
breast bone—scraping it!—This performed, while I
yet remained in utterly speechless torture, I heard
the Voice of Mr. Larry,—(all others guarded a dead
silence) in a tone nearly tragic, desire everyone present
to pronounce if any thing more remained to be done;
or if they thought the operation complete. The general
voice was Yes,—but the finger of Mr. Dubois—
which I literally felt elevated over the wound, though
I saw nothing, & though he touched nothing, so
indescribably sensitive was the spot—pointed to some
further requisition—& again began the scraping!—
and, after this, Dr. Moreau thought he discerned
a peccant attom—and still, & still, M. Dubois
demanded attom after attom.—My dearest Esther,
not for days, not for Weeks, but for Months I could
not speak of this terrible business without nearly
again going through it! I could not think of it with
impunity! I was sick, I was disordered by a single
question—even now, 9 months after it is over, I have

a head ache from going on with the account! & this
miserable account, which I began 3 Months ago, at
least, I dare not revise, nor read, the recollection is still
so painful.

To conclude, the evil was so profound, the case so
delicate, & the precautions necessary for preventing a
return so numerous, that the operation, including the
treatment and the dressing, lasted 20 minutes! a time,
for sufferings so acute, that was hardly supportable—
However, I bore it with all the courage I could
exert, & never moved, nor stopt them, nor resisted, nor
remonstrated, nor spoke—except once or twice. . . .
Twice, I believe, I fainted; at least, I have two total
chasms in my memory of this transaction, that impede
my tying together what passed. When all was done, &
they lifted me up that I might be put to bed, my
strength was so totally annihilated, that I was obliged
to be carried, & could not even sustain my hands &
arms, which hung as if I had been lifeless; while my
face, as the Nurse has told me, was utterly colorless.
This removal made me open my Eyes—& I then saw
my good Dr. Larry, pale nearly as myself, his face
streaked with blood, & its expression depicting grief,
apprehension, & almost horror.

David Hughes to his parents, 21 August 1940

Flight Lieutenant David Hughes was a pilot who served in the
Battle of Britain, the air war that prevented a Nazi invasion and
ensured British independence from Hitler's empire. The battle
was won by the young pilots of the RAF, often just eighteen

years old, many of whom were killed in the desperate fighting over England and the Channel. Posted near Newquay in Cornwall, Hughes's jaunty letter to his family tells of their excitements and fears.

It was Prime Minister Winston Churchill who best described the courage of those pilots in his famous speech: "The gratitude of every home in our island, in our empire, and indeed throughout the world, except in the abodes of the guilty, goes out to the British airmen who, undaunted by odds, unweakened by their constant challenge and mortal danger, are turning the tide of world war by their prowess and their devotion. Never in the field of human conflict was so much owed by so many to so few. All hearts go out to the fighter pilots."

Less than a month after this letter, on 11 September 1940, Hughes was shot down over the English Channel; his body was never recovered.

RAF ST. EVAL, NR NEWQUAY, CORNWALL, 21 AUGUST 1940:

My Darlings,
     It is a very long time since last I wrote, and very many things have happened.
     I have shot and been shot at. I have killed, but not been killed. I have had my life saved by a comrade, and saved another in return.
     I am now what is termed as an "Ace," in that I have over 5 Jerries to my credit, namely 6 machines have been destroyed through my pressing a little button. For the boys' information I have shot down 3 ME 110's, 2 ME 109's, and a Dornier 17.
     I arrived in my new Squadron on Sunday August 4th. There were three officers senior to me in

the Squadron then. By August 11th I was the C.O. We lost twelve pilots in 4 days. After I took over we only lost one in a week, and had even greater odds against us. One day we were the first Squadron to make contact with the enemy, and I led my Squadron, twelve of us, against 350 Bombers escorted by 400 enemy fighters. It was one HELL of a scrap. When I landed I had 150 bullet holes in my machine, one was ½" from my head. I said a quick prayer before we dived to the attack, and I think my guardian angel was working overtime!!

On the 18th August our Squadron was sent down here for a rest, and we needed it. I'd lost a stone in under a fortnight. We had been flying for 6 and seven hours a day, missing meals, and averaging 5 hours sleep a day!

When we got here I had a telegram which read "Congratulations 238 Squadron for the great part you have played" from Sir Cyril Newall, Air Chief Marshal.

Up to today we have had a quiet time here, but the Nazis gave us their attention today, and bombed us here. I was in the Mess when the bombs came, and rushed down to the machines and as I took off the Jerries machine gunned me, and then dodged into the clouds and got away.

I don't know when we shall return to Wallop, but I expect it will be soon.

I flew over to Cardiff last Monday and saw Joan [his wife] for a couple of hours. She has had a bad time recently, poor darling, her throat was bad again. I do love her so!!

I am writing this in flying kit and waiting for the word to take off.

Take care darlings.

All my love,
David.

Discovery

Ada Lovelace to Andrew Crosse,
c.16 November 1844

Ada Lovelace was born in 1815, the daughter of the "mad bad and dangerous to know" Romantic poet, Lord Byron. The poet had many illegitimate children, but Ada was the only child of his marriage to Annabel Millbank. His scandalous conduct and political liberalism forced him to leave England just four months after she was born, never to meet her again: "Is thy face like thy mother's, my fair child! ADA! sole daughter of my house and heart?" he wrote in *Childe Harold's Pilgrimage*. Byron died in Greece in 1824. Ada's mother denounced his many perversions and debaucheries for the rest of her life but showed little interest in Ada, who was brought up by her grand-mother. She suffered headaches and near paralysis after measles and dreamed of designing a flying machine to fly away in—and escape her illness.

She was always fascinated by mathematics and science, showing a precocious talent in an age when few women were educated, let alone brilliant scientists in their own right. She had an affair and almost eloped with her tutor William Turner when she was seventeen, but three years later in 1835 she married Lord King, who became the Earl of Lovelace—giving her the fantastical title Countess of Lovelace—and they had three children. Ada's most important relationship was with her friend and mentor Charles Babbage (who called her "Lady Fairy") and together they became pioneers of computing. Writing to her fellow scientist Andrew Crosse (with whose son John she probably had a love affair, beginning when he accompanied his father to the meeting referred to in this letter) from her home in Surrey, she calls herself "the bride of science," explaining her modern philosophy of the interconnectivity of all nature and talking of her usual ill health. Ada died at thirty-six from uterine cancer—the same age as her father, with whom she was buried.

Dear Mr. Crosse,—Thank you for your kind and cordial letter. . . . On Monday the 18th then, we expect you, and on Wednesday 20th we will all go to Broomfield. Perhaps you have felt already, from the tone of my letter, that I am more than ever now the bride of science. Religion to me is science, and science is religion. In that deeply-felt truth lies the secret of my intense devotion to the reading of God's natural works. . . . And when I behold the scientific and so-called philosophers full of selfish feelings, and of a tendency to war against circumstances and Providence, I say to myself: They are not true priests, they are but half prophets—if not absolutely false ones. They have read the great page simply with the physical eye, and with none of the spirit within. The intellectual, the moral, the religious seem to be all naturally bound up and interlinked together in one great and harmonious whole. . . . That God is one, and all that all the works and the feelings He has called into existence are ONE; this is a truth (a biblical and scriptural truth too) not in my opinion developed to the apprehension of most people in its really deep and unfathomable meaning. There is too much tendency to making separate and independent bundles of both the physical and the moral facts of the universe. Whereas, all and everything is naturally related and interconnected. A volume could I write on this subject. . . . I think I may as well just give you a hint that I am subject at times to dreadful physical sufferings. If such should come over me at Broomfield, I may have to keep to my room for a time. In that case all I require is to be let alone. With all my wiry power and strength, I am prone at times to bodily sufferings, connected chiefly with the digestive organs, of no common degree or kind. . . .

Ever yours truly,
AA Lovelace

Wilbur Wright to the Smithsonian Institution, 30 May 1899

A letter that flies. Enthusiasts of flight, not a pair of cranks, Wilbur Wright and his brother Orville were mechanics who produced their own brand of bicycle, but that was at many removes from an airplane. Yet they long dreamed of flight and practiced the mechanics in their shop. It still seems extraordinarily unlikely, but when Wright, aged thirty-two, writes this letter, he is only three years from the first controlled flight. . . .

THE SMITHSONIAN INSTITUTION,
WASHINGTON

Dear Sirs:
    I have been interested in the problem of mechanical and human flight ever since as a boy I constructed

a number of boats of various sizes after the style of Cayley's and Pénaud's machines. My observations since have only convinced me more firmly that human flight is possible and practicable. It is only a question of knowledge and skill just as in all acrobatic feats. Birds are the most perfectly trained gymnasts in the world and are specially well fitted for their work, and it may be that man will never equal them, but no one who has watched a bird chasing an insect or another bird can doubt that feats are performed which require three or four times the effort required in ordinary flight. I believe that simple flight at least is possible to man and that the experiments and investigations of a large number of independent workers will result in the accumulation of information and knowledge and skill which will finally lead to accomplished flight. . . .

I am an enthusiast, but not a crank in the sense that I have some pet theories as to the proper construction of a flying machine. I wish to avail myself of all that is already known and then if possible add my mite to help on the future workers who will attain final success. I do not know the terms on which you send out your publications but if you will inform me of the cost I will remit the price.

Yours truly
Wilbur Wright

John Stevens Henslow to Charles Darwin,
24 August 1831

One of the foundation theories of modern biology starts with this letter. Charles Darwin said of his friend the Reverend John Stevens Henslow: "I fully believe a better man never walked the earth." The two met at Cambridge University in 1828, where Henslow was the Regius Professor of Botany, and became sufficiently good friends that Darwin was known as "the man who walks with Henslow." When Henslow heard of a place on an expedition led by Captain Robert FitzRoy aboard HMS *Beagle* to South America for two years, he thought first of his protégé Darwin. The friend referred to in this letter, Marmaduke Ramsay, had proposed a trip to the Canary Islands, which Darwin would have attended had it not been for Ramsay's sudden death. This journey, which would last five years, gave Darwin the chance to research his ideas and led to his world-changing theory of evolution by natural selection, finally published in 1859 in *On the Origin of Species*.

My dear Darwin,
    Before I enter upon the immediate business of
this letter, let us condole together upon the loss of our
inestimable friend poor Ramsay of whose death you
have undoubtedly heard long before this. I will not now
dwell upon this painful subject as I shall hope to see
you shortly fully expecting that you will eagerly catch
at the offer which is likely to be made you of a trip to
Terra del Fuego & home by the East Indies—I have
been asked by Peacock who will read & forward this
to you from London to recommend him a naturalist as
companion to Capt FitzRoy employed by Government

to survey the S. extremity of America—I have stated
that I consider you to be the best qualified person I
know of who is likely to undertake such a situation—I
state this not on the supposition of yr. being a finished
Naturalist, but as amply qualified for collecting,
observing, & noting any thing worthy to be noted in
Natural History. Peacock has the appointment at his
disposal & if he can not find a man willing to take the
office, the opportunity will probably be lost—Capt. F.
wants a man (I understand) more as a companion than
a mere collector & would not take any one however
good a Naturalist who was not recommended to him
likewise as a gentleman. Particulars of salary &c I know
nothing. The Voyage is to last 2 yrs. & if you take plenty
of Books with you, any thing you please may be done—
You will have ample opportunities at command—In
short I suppose there never was a finer chance for a
man of zeal & spirit. Capt F. is a young man. What I
wish you to do is instantly to come to Town & consult
with Peacock (at No. 7 Suffolk Street Pall Mall East or
else at the University Club) & learn further particulars.
Don't put on any modest doubts or fears about your
disqualifications for I assure you I think you are the
very man they are in search of—so conceive yourself
to be tapped on the Shoulder by your Bum-Bailiff &
affecte friend

                                        J. S. Henslow

Ferdinand and Isabella, King and Queen of Castile and Aragon, to Christopher Columbus, 30 March 1493 and 29 April 1493

The letters that give Europeans their first glimpse of America. This marks the beginning of the age of empires in the Americas and their settlement by European colonists. The entire modern world starts with this letter accepting Spanish sovereignty. After much lobbying by the Genoan sailor and visionary Christopher Columbus, the "Most Catholic Monarchs" of Spain, Ferdinand and Isabella, had finally permitted him to set sail expecting to find a route to India. On 3 August 1492 he embarked with ninety men. The Most Catholic Monarchs heard nothing until March 1493 when they received word that although he had lost one ship he had indeed discovered the Indies, seen the mainland of Asia (which in fact was today's Cuba), and founded a settlement on the island of Hispaniola (now Haiti and the Dominican Republic). On 30 March they reply with this letter, urging him to return to the court in Barcelona:

Sir Christopher Columbus, our admiral of the Ocean Sea and viceroy and governor of the islands that have been discovered in the Indies. We have seen your letters and were very pleased to learn about what you wrote to us in them and also that God has given you such a good ending to your efforts, guiding you well in what you began, by which He and we will be well served and our kingdoms will receive great benefit. May it please God that, besides serving Him in this, you will also receive because of it many favors from us that, rest assured, will be conferred on you as your services and labors merit.

We wish you to continue and carry forward
what you have begun, with the help of God, and
thus desire that you return immediately, because it
is to our service that you hurry your return as much
as possible in order to supply everything needed on
time.

Christopher Columbus to Ferdinand and Isabella, 29 April 1493

Upon his return to Spain after his first voyage, Columbus
writes a letter detailing "the recently discovered Islands of India
beyond the Ganges," addressed to the royal treasurer but meant
for the monarchs Ferdinand and Isabella. It is later published.
Famed for the "discovery" of America, it was only new to Europeans: civilizations unknown to Europe had thrived there for
millennia. Columbus was correct though that the Carib people
were man-eating—and this letter describing them is the origin
of the word "cannibal." Columbus believes he has reached the
coast of China. Only Amerigo Vespucci later realized this was
the New World.

As I know that it will afford you pleasure that I have
brought my undertaking to a successful result, I
have determined to write you this letter to inform
you of everything that has been done and discovered
in this voyage of mine.
    On the thirty-third day after leaving Cadiz I
came into the Indian Sea, where I discovered many
islands inhabited by numerous people. I took possession
of all of them for our most fortunate King by making

public proclamation and unfurling his standard, no one making any resistance.

To the first of them I have given the name of our blessed Savior, with whose aid I have reached this and all the rest; but the Indians call it Guanahani. To each of the others also I gave a new name, ordering one to be called Sancta Maria de Concepcion, another Fernandina, another Isabella, another Juana; and so with all the rest. As soon as we reached the island which I have just said was called Juana, I sailed along its coast some considerable distance toward the West, and found it to be so large, without any apparent end, that I believed it was not an island, but a continent, a province of Cathay [China]. But I saw neither towns nor cities lying on the seaboard, only some villages and country farms, with whose inhabitants I could not get speech, because they fled as soon as they beheld us. I continued on, supposing I should come upon some city, or country-houses. At last, finding that no discoveries rewarded our further progress, and that this course was leading us toward the North, which I was desirous of avoiding, as it was now winter in these regions, and it had always been my intention to proceed Southwards, and the winds also were favorable to such desires, I concluded not to attempt any other adventures; so, turning back, I came again to a certain harbor, which I had remarked. From there I sent two of our men into the country to learn whether there was any king or cities in that land. They journeyed for three days, and found innumerable people and habitations, but small and having no fixed government; on which account they returned. Meanwhile I had learned from some

Indians, whom I had seized at this place, that this
country was really an island. . . .

In the island, which I have said before was called
Hispana, there are very lofty and beautiful mountains,
great farms, groves and fields, most fertile both for
cultivation and for pasturage, and well adapted for
constructing buildings. The convenience of the harbors
in this island, and the excellence of the rivers, in volume
and salubrity, surpass human belief, unless one should
see them. . . . Besides, this Hispana abounds in various
kinds of species, gold and metals. The inhabitants of
both sexes of this and of all the other islands I have
seen, or of which I have any knowledge, always go as
naked as they came into the world, except that some
of the women cover their private parts with leaves
or branches, or a veil of cotton, which they prepare
themselves for this purpose. They are all, as I said
before, unprovided with any sort of iron, and they are
destitute of arms, which are entirely unknown to them,
and for which they are not adapted; not on account
of any bodily deformity, for they are well made, but
because they are timid and full of terror. They carry,
however, canes dried in the sun in place of weapons,
upon whose roots they fix a wooded shaft, dried and
sharpened to a point. But they never dare to make use
of these; for it has often happened, when I have sent
two or three of my men to some of their villages to
speak with the inhabitants, that a crowd of Indians has
sallied forth; but when they saw our men approaching,
they speedily took to flight, parents abandoning
children, and children their parents. This happened not
because any loss or injury had been inflicted upon any
of them. On the contrary I gave whatever I had, cloth

and many other things, to whomsoever I approached, or with whom I could get speech, without any return being made to me; but they are by nature fearful and timid. But when they see that they are safe, and all fear is banished, they are very guileless and honest, and very liberal of all they have. No one refuses the asker anything that he possesses; on the contrary they themselves invite us to ask for it. They manifest the greatest affection toward all of us, exchanging valuable things for trifles, content with the very least thing or nothing at all. But I forbade giving them a very trifling thing and of no value, such as bits of plates, dishes, or glass; also nails and straps; although it seemed to them, if they could get such, that they had acquired the most beautiful jewels in the world . . . for pieces of hoops, jugs, jars, and pots they bartered cotton and gold like beasts. This I forbade, because it was plainly unjust; and I gave them many beautiful and pleasing things, which I had brought with me, for no return whatever, in order to win their affection, and that they might become Christians and inclined to love our King and Queen and Princes and all the people of Spain; and that they might be eager to search for and gather and give to us what they abound in and we greatly need. . . .

As soon as I had some into this sea, I took by force some Indians from the first island, in order that they might learn from us, and at the same time tell us what they knew about affairs in these regions. This succeeded admirably; for in a short time we understood them and they us both by gesture and signs and words; and they were of great service to us. They are coming now with me, and have always believed that I have come from Heaven, notwithstanding the long time they have

been, and still remain, with us. They were the first who
told this wherever we went, one calling to another,
with a loud voice, Come, Come, you will see Men from
Heaven. Whereupon both women and men, children
and adults, young and old, laying aside the fear they
had felt a little before, flocked eagerly to see us, a great
crowd thronging about our steps, some bringing food,
and others drink, with greatest love and incredible good
will. . . .

I saw no monsters, neither did I hear accounts of
any such except in an island called Carib, the second as
one crosses over from Spain to India, which is inhabited
by a certain race regarded by their neighbors as very
ferocious. They eat human flesh, and make use of
several kinds of boats by which they cross over to all the
Indian islands, and plunder and carry off whatever they
can. But they differ in no respect from the others except
in wearing their hair long after the fashion of women.
They make use of bows and arrows made of reeds,
having pointed shafts fastened to the thicker portion,
as we have before described. For this reason they are
considered to be ferocious, and the other Indians
consequently are terribly afraid of them; but I consider
them of no more account than the others. They have
intercourse with certain women who dwell alone upon
the island of Mateurin, the first as one crosses from
Spain to India. These women follow none of the usual
occupations of their sex; but they use bows and arrows
like those of their husbands, which I have described,
and protect themselves with plates of copper, which is
found in the greatest abundance among them. . . .

Although these matters are very wonderful and
unheard of, they would have been much more so,

if ships to a reasonable amount had been furnished me. But what has been accomplished is great and wonderful, and not at all proportionate to my deserts, but to the sacred Christian faith, and to the piety and religion of our Sovereigns. For what is the mind of man could not compass the spirit of God has granted to mortals. . . .

Therefore let King and Queen and Princes, and their most fortunate realms, and all other Christian provinces, let us all return thanks to our Lord and Savior Jesus Christ, who has bestowed so great a victory and reward upon us . . . and let us be glad not only for the exaltation of our faith, but also for the increase of temporal prosperity, in which not only Spain but all Christendom is about to share.

As these things have been accomplished so have they been briefly narrated.

Farewell.

Tourism

Anton Chekhov to Anatoly Koni, 16 January 1891

In 1890 Anton Chekhov, a medical doctor as well as a celebrated writer, set off to the penal colony of Sakhalin in the
Russian Far East, to conduct a census of its prisoners. His letters from there record the suffering and degeneracy of these
godforsaken unfortunates and his own adventures, observing
humanity with a world-weary and humorous sensitivity and a
forensic precision.

To reach the "Hell of Sakhalin," Chekhov travels by ship,
river steamer, train, and carriage. On the way he records the
one-horse towns of the Far East. In one letter to his publisher
Alexander Suvorin, he describes a visit to the brothel in Blago-
veshchensk: "a nice clean room sentimental in an Asiatic way
furnished with bric-a-brac. . . . The Japanese girl has her own
concept of modesty. She doesn't put out the light and when you
ask what the Japanese is for one thing or another she gives a
straight answer as she does so because she doesn't understand
much Russian, points her fingers, and even puts her hand on it.
What's more she doesn't put on airs or go all coy like Russian
women. And all the time she is laughing. . . . She is amazingly skilled at her job so that you feel you are not having intercourse but taking part in a top level equitation class. When you
come, the Japanese girl pulls with her teeth a sheet of cotton
wool from her sleeve, catches you by the 'boy,' gives you a mas-

sage. . . . All this is done with coquetry, laughing, singing and saying tsu."

Born in Taganrog on the Sea of Azov, Chekhov had endured a hard childhood, but after qualifying as a doctor he started to write stories for Suvorin's newspaper. He became even more famous for plays like *The Cherry Orchard* and *Uncle Vanya,* describing the key to the art of drama: "Remove everything that has no relevance to the story. If you say in the first chapter that there is a rifle hanging on the wall, in the second or third chapter it absolutely must go off. If it's not going to be fired, it shouldn't be hanging there." After a raffish love life, forswearing marriage, he married late—but was only forty-four when he died of tuberculosis. He liked to claim "medicine is my wife, literature is my mistress," but this letter to his friend and lawyer Koni combines the two—it is one of his best.

DEAR SIR, ANATOLY FYODOROVITCH [KONI]

I did not hasten to answer your letter because I am not leaving Petersburg before next Saturday. I am sorry I have not been to see Madame Naryshkin, but I think I had better defer my visit till my book has come out, when I shall be able to turn more freely to the material I have. My brief Sakhalin past looms so immense in my imagination that when I want to speak about it I don't know where to begin, and it always seems to me that I have not said what was wanted.

I will try and describe minutely the position of the children and young people in Sakhalin. It is exceptional. I saw starving children, I saw girls of thirteen prostitutes, girls of fifteen with child. Girls begin to live by prostitution from twelve years old, sometimes before menstruation has begun. Church and school exist only on paper, the children are educated by their environment and the convict surroundings. Among other things I have noted down a conversation with a boy of ten years old. I was making the census of the settlement of Upper Armudano; all the inhabitants are poverty-stricken, every one of them, and have the reputation of being desperate gamblers at the game of shtoss. I go into a hut; the people are not at home; on a bench sits a white-haired, round-shouldered, barefooted boy; he seems lost in thought. We begin to talk.

I. "What is your father's second name?"

He. "I don't know."

I. "How is that? You live with your father and don't know what his name is? Shame!"

He. "He is not my real father."

I. "How is that?"

He. "He is living with mother."

I. "Is your mother married or a widow?"

He. "A widow. She followed her husband here."

I. "What has become of her husband, then?"

He. "She killed him."

I. "Do you remember your father?"

He. "No, I don't, I am illegitimate. I was born when mother was at Kara."

On the Amur steamer going to Sakhalin, there was a convict with fetters on his legs who had murdered his wife. His daughter, a little girl of six, was with him. I noticed wherever the convict moved the little girl scrambled after him, holding on to his fetters. At night the child slept with the convicts and soldiers all in a heap together. I remember I was at a funeral in Sakhalin. Beside the newly dug grave stood four convict bearers ex officio; the treasury clerk and I, in the capacity of Hamlet and Horatio, wandering about the cemetery; the dead woman's lodger, a Circassian, who had come because he had nothing better to do; and a convict woman who had come out of pity and had brought the dead woman's two children, one a baby, and the other, Alyoshka, a boy of four, wearing a woman's jacket and blue breeches with bright colored patches on the knees. It was cold and damp, there was water in the grave, the convicts were laughing. The sea was in sight. Alyoshka looked into the grave with curiosity; he tried to wipe his chilly nose, but the long sleeve of his jacket got into his way. When they began to fill in the grave I asked him: "Alyoshka, where is your mother?" He waved his hand with the air of a gentleman who has lost at cards, laughed, and said: "They have buried her!"

The convicts laughed, the Circassian turned and asked what he was to do with the children, saying it was not his duty to feed them.

Infectious diseases I did not meet with in Sakhalin. There is very little congenital syphilis, but I saw blind children, filthy, covered with eruptions—all diseases that are evidence of neglect. Of course I am not going to settle the problem of the children. I don't know what ought to be done.

Gustave Flaubert to Louis Bouilhet, 15 January 1850

This letter of sexual adventure is by Gustave Flaubert, the French novelist, to his school friend and fellow writer Louis Bouilhet. In 1849–50, aged around thirty, Flaubert travels through the Middle East, from Greece to Istanbul and Beirut, sightseeing and experiencing as much as he could in the backstreets and bathhouses. His letters describe encounters with girls and boys, joking that he travels for "educational purposes." His risky adventures cost him dear—he was tormented for the rest of his life by the infections he contracted there and this contributed to his decision not to marry or have children.

On his return, he started work on his masterpiece, *Madame Bovary,* the story of a disastrous, adulterous affair. He prided himself on his search for the precise word in his writing—"le mot juste"—exhausting himself with this exacting perfectionism that meant he published many fewer works than his equals, Balzac and Zola. But even in this letter, set in a Cairo bathhouse, the wit is as acute as the style is meticulous.

> . . . Speaking of bardashes, this is what I know
> about them. Here it is quite accepted. One admits
> one's sodomy, and it is spoken of at table in the
> hotel. Sometimes you do a bit of denying, and then
> everybody teases you and you end up confessing.
> Traveling as we are for educational purposes, and
> charged with a mission by the government, we have
> considered it our duty to indulge in this form of
> ejaculation. So far the occasion has not presented
> itself. We continue to seek it, however. It's at the baths

that such things take place. You reserve the bath for yourself (five francs including masseurs, pipe, coffee, sheet and towel) and you skewer your lad in one of the rooms. Be informed, furthermore, that all the bath-boys are bardashes. The final masseurs, the ones who come to rub you when all the rest is done, are usually quite nice young boys. We had our eye on one in an establishment very near our hotel. I reserved the bath exclusively for myself. I went, and the rascal was away that day! I was alone in the hot room, watching the daylight fade through the great circles of glass in the dome. Hot water was flowing everywhere; stretched out indolently I thought of a quantity of things as my pores tranquilly dilated. It is very voluptuous and sweetly melancholy to take a bath like that quite alone, lost in those dim rooms where the slightest noise reverberates like cannon shot, while the naked kellaks call out to one another as they massage you, turning you over like embalmers preparing you for the tomb. That day (the day before yesterday, Monday), my kellak was rubbing me gently, and when he came to the noble parts he lifted up my boules d'amour to clean them, then continuing to rub my chest with his left hand, he began to pull with his right on my prick, and as he drew it up and down, he leaned over my shoulder and said "baksheesh, baksheesh." He was a man in his fifties, ignoble, disgusting—imagine the effect, and the word "baksheesh, baksheesh." I pushed him away a little, saying "làh, làh" ("no, no")—he thought I was angry and took on a craven look—then I gave him a few pats on the shoulder, saying "làh, làh" again but more gently—he smiled a smile that meant "You're not fooling me—you like it as much as anybody, but today you've decided against it for some reason." As for me, I laughed aloud like a dirty old man and the shadowy vault of the bath echoed with the sound. . . .

War

Peter the Great to Catherine I, 27 June 1709

This letter marks the moment that Russia becomes a world power—the triumph every Russian leader from Stalin to Putin aspires to emulate. Peter the Great was the six-foot-seven tsar who, in 1707, faced an invasion from the best army of the day, Sweden. But he fought back, founded a new capital—St. Petersburg—and created a new navy and army. Finally, on this day in 1709 at Poltava, he defeats the Swedes and wants to share the moment with his wife.

She too is an extraordinary individual. She had been a laundress, mistress of many generals, and was not even a Russian; but Peter fell in love with her, changed her name to Catherine, and ultimately would make her empress of Russia in her own right. In their saucy letters he calls her "Katerinushka, my heart's friend," often adding "I am bored without you." They would tease each other about other girls—especially laundresses. "I got your letter full of jokes. You'll say I'll be looking for a new lady but I am too old," he writes to her when visiting Versailles on 28 April 1717.

"I think Your Worship is distracted by a multitude of fountains and forgets us," she jokes back on 25 May, with much phallic imagery. "Though I think you have found new laundresses, your old laundress hasn't forgotten you."

Joshing about sex and his frequent affliction, venereal disease, he remarks, "The doctors ban domestic fun. I've sent my mistress away for I won't be able to resist the temptation if I kept her here." To which Catherine replies, "I hope the mistress's admirer [Peter] will arrive in the same state of health as she did!" adding, "But if my old man was here we'd make us another kid." They had around twelve children together but all the boys died. On 2 January 1717 he celebrates a new son: "I received your delightful letter in which you say the Lord God has blessed us by giving us another recruit." The very next day, hearing the baby has died, he tries to console his wife: "I received your letter about what I knew before, the unexpected occurrence which has changed joy to grief. What answer can I give except that of the long-suffering Job? The Lord has given and the Lord has taken away; Blessed be the name of the Lord. I beg you to reflect on it in this way; I do as far as I can."

So this partner is the person with whom he wishes to share his world-changing victory at Poltava, writing to her:

Matushka, good day. I declare to you that the
all-merciful God has this day granted us an
unprecedented victory over the enemy. In a word, the
whole of the enemy's army is knocked on the head,
about which you will hear from us.

Peter

PS Come here and congratulate us!

Napoleon to Josephine, 3 December 1805

This is the letter of a man who has just defeated the emperors of Russia and Austria and is now the master of Europe. On the battlefield of Austerlitz, Napoleon scribbles the following note to his wife, Josephine.

> To the Empress, at Strasbourg,
> I have sent Lebrun to you from the battlefield. I defeated the Russian and Austrian army commanded by the two emperors. I am slightly [!] tired, as I spent eight days in a bivouac out in the open and the nights were rather cold. Tonight, I am staying at the palace of Prince Kaunitz, where I shall sleep two or three hours. The Russian army is not only defeated, it is destroyed.
>
> *I kiss you,*
> Napoleon.

Dwight D. Eisenhower to all Allied troops, 5 June 1944

On 5 June 1944 General "Ike" Eisenhower, supreme allied commander of the Allied Expeditionary Force and later president of the United States, gives the order to launch the long-awaited Operation Overlord, the invasion of Nazi-occupied France. It is risky: an assault across the Channel with overwhelming force but against the well-defended coast of Hitler's Atlantic Wall—and at the mercy of weather and sea and Nazi airpower. On that day Eisenhower writes one letter to be issued to all the troops before the assault. But he also writes a second one, to be issued in the event of a disaster, wrongly dated 5 July. Fortunately, this letter was never sent. D-Day was successful. Here is the first:

You are about to embark upon a great crusade, toward which we have striven these many months. The eyes of the world are upon you. . . . We will accept nothing less than full victory! Good Luck!

And this is the letter never sent:

5 JULY

Our landings in the Cherbourg-Havre area have failed to gain a satisfactory foothold and I have withdrawn the troops. My decision to attack at this time and place was based upon the best information available. The troops, the air and the Navy did all that Bravery and devotion to duty could do. If any blame or fault attaches to the attempt it is mine alone.

Catherine, Duchess of Oldenburg, to her brother Alexander I, 3 September 1812

In the summer of 1812, the French emperor Napoleon invaded Russia. By September he had taken the ancient capital of Moscow, which was then burned to the ground, a shocking humiliation for Tsar Alexander I and the Russian people. At this moment of disaster, Alexander trusts no one and knows his reputation, if not his actual life, is in peril. He is encouraged in his determination to resist at all costs—even if he has to retreat all the way back to the city of Kazan—by the person he loves most of all: his strong and fearless sister Catiche. This letter is as powerful as it is short.

Moscow is taken. Some things are beyond
comprehension. Don't forget your resolve, "no peace,"
and you have still the hope of regaining your honor.
If you are in sorrow don't forget your friends ready to
fly to you and too happy if they can be any help:
command them.

My dear friend, no peace, and if you get to Kazan,
still no peace!

Philip II to the Duke of Medina Sidonia, 1 July 1588

A letter encouraging a reluctant servant to perform a thankless
task of extraordinary magnitude.

Philip of Spain was the most powerful king in Europe
at the time, ruler of an empire on which the sun never set—
but Queen Elizabeth of England defied him. First he had
asked her to marry him, then he ordered her assassination,
and finally he contrived his Great Enterprise: the invasion
of England by his "Great and Most Fortunate Navy"—the
Spanish Armada—carrying 27,000 men in a hundred and
thirty warships that were to collect en route, as the invasion
force, a further 30,000 waiting in the Spanish Netherlands.
Philip gave the command to an experienced admiral, the
Marqués de Santa Cruz, but he died before the fleet set off,
and the king ordered the Duke of Medina Sidonia to take
his place. The duke, no sailor, knew the plan was faulty, so he
tried to back out: "Your Majesty, believe me when I assure
you that we are very weak . . . how do you think we can
attack so great a country as England with such a force as ours
is now?"

This is Philip's reply. The armada sailed on 28 May 1588 and was a disaster.

> Duke and cousin.
>   I have received the letter written in your hand, dated 24 June. From what I know of you, I believe you have brought all these matters to my attention solely because of your zeal to serve me and the desire to succeed in your command. The certainty that this is so prompts me to be franker with you than I should be with another. . . . If this were an unjust war, one could indeed take the tempest as a sign from Our Lord to cease offending Him; but being as just as it is, one cannot believe that He will disband it, but will rather grant it more favor than we could hope. . . . I have dedicated this enterprise to God. . . . Pull yourself together, then, and do your part.
>   Philip.

Harun al-Rashid to Nikephoros I, AD 802

Harun al-Rashid was the fifth and most famous Abbasid caliph—formally the Emir al-Muamimin, or Commander of the Faithful, ruling the vast Islamic empire from Baghdad. He is the caliph who appears in *The Thousand and One Nights*. When he is defied by the Byzantine emperor Nikephoros, who refuses to pay tribute, the caliph sends this laconic reply—promising war.

> In the name of God, the Merciful, the Compassionate, from Harun the Commander of the Faithful to

Nikephoros the dog of the Byzantines: O son of an
infidel woman, I have read your letter, and the reply
is what you will see, without you having to hear it.
Farewell!

Rasputin to Nicholas II, 17 July 1914

Perhaps the most outspoken letter ever written to a tsar by a
peasant. In July 1914, Europe slides toward war. Tsar Nicholas is
reluctant to fight, yet fears that Russia cannot avoid conflict and
remain a great power. His wife, Alexandra, is with him but he
excludes her from discussions, fearing her hysteria. Their sacred
adviser, the peasant Rasputin, is far from the capital, recovering
from an attempt to kill him, but when Alexandra discovers Russia is close to war, she telegraphs him, begging him to appeal to
the tsar. This is the letter Rasputin sends by telegram, warning
of catastrophe if Russia should fight. Nicholas was outraged by
Rasputin's impertinence—yet he was right. And Nicholas kept
the letter until his own murder in 1918.

Dear friend
    I'll say again a menacing cloud is over Russia, lots
of sorrow and grief, it's dark and there's not a ray of
hope. A sea of tears, immeasurable, and as to blood?
What can I say? There are no words, indescribable
horror. I know they all want war from you, evidently
not realizing that this means ruin. Hard is God's
punishment when he takes away reason, it's the
beginning of the end. You are the Tsar Father of
the people, don't allow the madmen to triumph and
destroy themselves and the people. Yes, they'll conquer

Germany, but what of Russia? If one thinks then truly never for all of time has one suffered like Russia, drowned in her own blood. Great will be the ruin, grief without end.

Grigory

Blood

Paiankh to Nodjmet, c.1070 BC

Murder by letter. The military dictator of Thebes, Paiankh ruled with his wife, Nodjmet. In an early case of state killing, while Paiankh is away fighting rebellious Nubia, he has left his wife, Nodjmet, in charge. When she senses treason at home she asks his advice. Paiankh's reply is unequivocal and chilling: disappear them!

> Have these two watchmen brought to my house and get to the bottom of their words in short order, then have them killed and thrown into the water by night.

Vladimir Lenin to the Bolsheviks of Penza, 11 August 1918

Here is the real Lenin as the Soviet people never saw him.

Vladimir Lenin became Soviet premier when he led the Bolshevik seizure of power in October 1917. During his rule and after his death he was promoted in propaganda as a benign grandfatherly patriarch, his body preserved and revered in a mausoleum like a saint. On the contrary, Lenin prided himself on his harshness and often said, "A revolution without firing squads is meaningless." When he heard that Stalin had killed people he said, "That's exactly the type we need." As soon as Lenin took power he created the ruthless Cheka, the secret police, to enforce his terror; and as his regime struggles to win the civil war, he sends letters like this, ordering random killings. This letter was only revealed after the fall of the Soviet Union in 1991. His body still remains on show in Red Square.

Comrades! The insurrection of five kulak districts should be <u>pitilessly</u> suppressed. The interests of the <u>whole</u> revolution require this because "the last decisive battle" with the kulaks is now underway <u>everywhere</u>. An example must be demonstrated.

1. Hang (and make sure that the hanging takes place <u>in full view of the people) no fewer than one hundred</u> known kulaks, rich men, bloodsuckers.
2. Publish their names.
3. Seize <u>all</u> their grain from them.
4. Designate hostages in accordance with yesterday's telegram.

Do it in such a fashion that for hundreds of kilometers around the people might see, tremble, know, shout: <u>they are strangling</u> and will strangle to death the bloodsucking kulaks.

Telegraph receipt and <u>implementation</u>.

Yours, Lenin.

Find some truly hard people.

Josef Stalin to Kliment Voroshilov, 3 July 1937

In February 1937, Stalin unleashed the Great Terror, directed mainly at his own comrades in the Communist Party. Around a million innocent people were eventually shot, millions more imprisoned. In public he remains elusive as the arrests and executions intensify, but privately he is directing every detail, and many of his letters to his henchmen, encouraging the slaughter, survive: "Isn't it time to squeeze this gentleman and force him to report on this dirty business?" he writes during the torture of one prisoner. At other times he sends peremptory letters like this one to a trusted acolyte: "Comrade Malenkov. Moskvin must be arrested. J.St." When his killers become exhausted, he urges them on: "The sharper the teeth the better. J.St."

He convinces his comrades that the arrested are guilty by showing them confessions, secured by torture. Here he sends these testimonies to a henchman with this covering letter:

> Dear Klim, did you read the testimonies . . . ? How
> do you like the bourgeois puppies of Trotsky . . . ?
> They wanted to wipe out all the members of the
> Politburo . . . isn't it weird? How low can people sink?
> J.St.

Mao Zedong to the Red Guards of Tsinghua University Middle School, 1 August 1966

Here is the letter unleashing the chaos and cruelty of the Cultural Revolution. Since seizing power in 1949, Mao had killed millions of "class enemies" by shooting and by famine but now, directing a campaign behind the scenes backed by henchmen like his wife, Jiang Qing, and his defense minister, Lin Biao, Mao turns the guns on his own over-mighty officials who had tried to restrain his power. His weapons are the young student radicals and thugs of the Red Guards, whom he uses to destroy any rivals by inciting mob violence or, as he calls it, "bombarding the headquarters."

This letter is one of the public signs of his support for the Red Guards: "it is right to rebel against reactionaries." He suggests that "after their mistakes have been pointed out," their victims should be offered the chance to become "new men." This is sinister double-talk: many were tortured, killed, or "re-educated" in the countryside.

Red Guard Comrades

I have received both the big-character posters which you sent on 28 July as well as the letter which you sent me, asking for an answer. The big-character posters express your anger at and denunciation of all landlords, bourgeois, imperialists, revisionists and their running dogs who exploit and oppress the workers, peasants, revolutionary intellectuals and revolutionary parties and groupings. You say it is right to rebel against reactionaries: I enthusiastically support you. . . . Here I want to say that I myself as well as my revolutionary comrades-in-arms all take the same attitude. No matter where they are, in Peking or anywhere in China, I will give enthusiastic support to all who take an attitude similar to yours in the Cultural Revolution movement. Another thing, while supporting you, at the same time we ask you to pay attention to uniting with all who can be united with. As for those who have committed serious mistakes, after their mistakes have been pointed out you should offer them a way out of their difficulties by giving them work to do, and enabling them to correct their mistakes and become new men. Marx said: the proletariat must emancipate not only itself but all mankind. If it cannot emancipate all mankind, then

the proletariat itself will not be able to achieve final
emancipation. Will comrades please pay attention to
this truth too.

China descended into four years of state-sanctioned anar-
chy, with Chairman Mao emerging omnipotent. He promoted
Lin Biao as his chosen heir, but then he started to turn on his
second-in-command. Marshal Lin planned Mao's assassination
before attempting to flee to Russia and was killed on 13 September 1971 when his plane crashed. In the ensuing search for
enemies, Mao wrote this short note advising deputy chief body-
guard Zhang Yao-ci how to survive. The reference to "operas and
films" shows Mao withdrawing support from his radical wife
Jiang Qing, who controlled the arts—and ending the Cultural
Revolution. The letter reveals the bleak state of paranoia and
terror at the court of one of the twentieth century's monsters—
in his own words.

1. Don't cultivate connections;
2. Don't visit people;
3. Don't give dinners or gifts;
4. Don't invite people to operas or films;
5. Don't have photographs taken with people.

Josip Broz Tito to Josef Stalin, 1948

The letter that terrified the most terrifying leader of modern
times. When a schism grows between the Communist allies—the
Soviet Union and Yugoslavia—Soviet leader Stalin expects the
smaller country to bow before his power. Instead, the Yugo-
slav president Marshal Tito defies Stalin, who is incensed. He
sends assassins to murder Tito, but they repeatedly fail. Finally

the Yugoslavian sends this note to Stalin, who supposedly kept it with a few other special letters in his personal safe where it was found after his death. It worked. Stalin stopped sending assassins.

> Stop sending people to kill me! We've already captured five of them one of them with a bomb and another with a rifle. . . . If you don't stop sending killers, I'll send a very fast working one to Moscow and I certainly won't have to send another.

Destruction

Theobald von Bethmann-Hollweg to
Count Leopold Berchtold, 6 July 1914

This is the letter that launches the slaughter of the First World War. Reading its mannered language from the age of emperors and courts, it is hard to grasp the killing machine that it unleashed. Germany deserves blame, but Austria, Serbia, and Russia also share that responsibility. On 28 June 1914, Serbian terrorists, secretly backed by the Serbian government, kill Archduke Franz Ferdinand, heir to the Austro-Hungarian throne. In retaliation, Austria wishes to destroy Serbia, but the latter is backed by Russia, and Russia is backed France—and they are both backed by Britain. Many Austrian and German potentates believe that war would deliver the best chance to defeat Russia, but Austria cannot risk it without the support of its more powerful German ally. Austrian Foreign Secretary Leopold Berchtold agrees with his master Emperor Franz Josef that Serbian destruction is essential.

On 5 July, Berchtold sends his chief of staff Count Alexander von Hoyos to Berlin to get German backing. At lunch with the German kaiser Wilhelm II, the Austrian ambassador delivers Franz Josef's letter that argues "the attack on my poor nephew" was "no longer an affair at Sarajevo of the single bloody deed of an individual but a well-organized conspiracy of which the threads lead to Belgrade." The kaiser promises Germany's "faithful support" even if Russia intervenes, a policy confirmed by his chancellor, Bethmann-Hollweg, in this letter: the early paragraphs concern Austria's wish to move away from Romania (ruled by a king closely related to the German kaiser) but the last two lines are decisive—the so-called Blank Check. The Germans grossly underestimate the Russian determination to defend Serbia, the French and British determination to back the Russians, and finally the British determination to back their French and Russian allies. By the time the Germans realize the scale of their miscalculation, it is too late. The war, which began on 28 July, would kill around 16 million people.

CONFIDENTIAL—FOR YOUR EXCELLENCY'S
PERSONAL INFORMATION AND GUIDANCE

BERLIN
6 JULY 1914

The Austro-Hungarian Ambassador yesterday delivered to the Emperor a confidential personal letter from the Emperor Francis Joseph, which depicts the present situation from the Austro-Hungarian point of view, and describes the measures which Vienna has in view. . . .

I replied to Count Szagyeny today on behalf of His Majesty that His Majesty sends his thanks to the Emperor Francis Joseph for his letter and would soon answer it personally.

In the meantime His Majesty desires to say that he is not blind to the danger which threatens Austria-Hungary and thus the Triple Alliance as a result of the Russian and Serbian Pan-Slavic agitation.

Even though His Majesty is known to feel no unqualified confidence in Bulgaria and her ruler, and

naturally inclines more toward our old ally Romania
and her Hohenzollern prince, yet he quite understands
that the Emperor Francis Joseph, in view of the attitude
of Romania and of the danger of a new Balkan alliance
aimed directly at the Danube Monarchy, is anxious to
bring about an understanding between Bulgaria and the
Triple Alliance.

   . . .

His Majesty will, furthermore, make an effort
at Bucharest, according to the wishes of the
Emperor Francis Joseph, to influence King Carol
to the fulfilment of the duties of his alliance, to the
renunciation of Serbia, and to the suppression of the
Romanian agitations directed against Austria-Hungary.

Finally, as far as concerns Serbia, His Majesty, of
course, cannot interfere in the dispute now going on
between Austria-Hungary and that country, as it is a
matter not within his competence.

The Emperor Francis Joseph may, however, rest
assured that His Majesty will faithfully stand by
Austria-Hungary, as is required by the obligations of
his alliance and of his ancient friendship.

                                      Bethmann-Hollweg

Harry Truman to Irv Kupcinet, 5 August 1963

President Harry Truman ordered the use of America's new
nuclear bombs to accelerate the end of the war against Japan.
On 6 and 9 August 1945, the atomic bombs dropped on
Hiroshima and then Nagasaki—causing a vast loss of life—
successfully forced Japan to sue for peace. They also heralded

the start of a new and terrifying era of nuclear proliferation, intensifying in the twenty-first century as less stable states such as Pakistan and North Korea become nuclear powers. Never has the fear of nuclear apocalypse been so real. That makes this letter by the retired president feel very relevant. The then seventy-nine-year-old Truman, living in retirement in Missouri, writes to the columnist Irv "Kup" Kupcinet, who has published an article supporting his actions in the *Chicago Sun-Times*. The letter reveals the matter-of-fact, no-nonsense style of the unpretentious ex-haberdasher who, as president, kept a sign on his desk that read: THE BUCK STOPS HERE.

Dear Kup:

I appreciated most highly your column of July 30th, a copy of which you sent me.

I have been rather careful not to comment on the articles that have been written on the dropping of the bomb for the simple reason that the dropping of the bomb was completely and thoroughly explained in my Memoirs, and it was done to save 125,000 youngsters on the American side and 125,000 on the Japanese side from getting killed and that is what it did. It probably also saved a half million youngsters on both sides from being maimed for life.

You must always remember that people forget, as you said in your column, that the bombing of Pearl Harbor was done while we were at peace with Japan and trying our best to negotiate a treaty with them. All you have to do is to go out and stand on the keel of the Battleship in Pearl Harbor with the 3,000 youngsters underneath it who had no chance whatever of saving their lives. That is true of two or three other battleships that were sunk in Pearl Harbor. Altogether, there were between 3,000 and 6,000 youngsters killed at that time without any declaration of war. It was plain murder.

I knew what I was doing when I stopped the war that would have killed a half million youngsters on both sides if those bombs had not been dropped. I have no regrets and, under the same circumstances, I would do it again—and this letter is not confidential.

Sincerely yours,
Harry Truman

Disaster

Pliny the Younger to Tacitus, c.AD 106–107

On 24 August AD 79 Mount Vesuvius erupted, destroying the nearby towns of Pompeii and Herculaneum entirely. The lawyer and writer Pliny the Younger was eighteen years old at the time of the eruption, which resulted in the death of his uncle Pliny the Elder. Young Pliny and his mother managed to escape. Around a quarter of a century later, Pliny's friend, the historian Tacitus, asks him to supply details of the event. Pliny's letter is a masterpiece of reportage.

You ask me to send you an account of my uncle's death, so that you may be able to give posterity an accurate description of it. I am much obliged to you, for I can see that the immortality of his fame is well assured, if you take in hand to write of it. For although he perished in a disaster which devastated some of the fairest regions of the land, and though he is sure of eternal remembrance like the peoples and cities that fell with him in that memorable calamity, though too he had written a large number of works of lasting value, yet the undying fame of which your writings are assured will secure for him a still further lease of life. For my own part, I think that those people are highly favored by Providence who are capable either of performing deeds worthy of the historian's pen or of writing histories worthy of being read, but that they are peculiarly favored who can do both. Among the latter I may class my uncle, thanks to his own writings and to yours. So I am all the more ready to fulfil your injunctions, nay, I am even prepared to beg to be allowed to undertake them.

My uncle was stationed at Misenum, where he was in active command of the fleet, with full powers. On the 24th of August, about the seventh hour, my mother drew his attention to the fact that a cloud of unusual size and shape had made its appearance. He had been out in the sun, followed by a cold bath, and after a light meal he was lying down and reading. Yet he called for his sandals, and climbed up to a spot from which he could command a good view of the curious phenomenon. Those who were looking at the cloud from some distance could not make out from which mountain it was rising—it was afterward discovered to have been Mount Vesuvius—but in likeness and form it more closely resembled a pine-tree than anything else, for what corresponded to the trunk was of great length and height, and then spread out into a number of branches, the reason being, I imagine, that while the vapor was fresh, the cloud was borne upward, but when the vapor became wasted, it lost its motion, or even became dissipated by its own weight, and spread out laterally. At times it looked white, and at other times dirty and spotted, according to the quantity of earth and cinders that were shot up.

To a man of my uncle's learning, the phenomenon appeared one of great importance, which deserved a closer study. He ordered a Liburnian galley to be got ready, and offered to take me with him, if I desired to accompany him, but I replied that I preferred to go on with my studies, and it so happened that he had assigned me some writing to do. He was just leaving the house when he received a written message from Rectina, the wife of Tascus, who was terrified at the peril threatening her—for her villa lay just beneath the mountain, and there were no means of escape save by shipboard—begging him to save her from her perilous position. So he changed his plans, and carried out with the greatest fortitude the task, which he had started as a scholarly inquiry.

He had the galleys launched and went on board himself, in the hope of succoring, not only Rectina, but many others, for there were a number of people living along the shore owing to its delightful situation. He hastened, therefore, toward the place whence others were fleeing, and steering a direct course, kept the helm straight for the point of danger, so utterly devoid of fear that every movement of the looming portent and every change in its appearance he described and had noted down by his secretary, as soon as his eyes detected it. Already ashes were beginning to fall upon the ships, hotter and in thicker showers as they approached more nearly, with pumice-stones and black flints, charred and cracked by the heat of the flames, while their way was barred by the sudden shoaling of the sea bottom and the litter of the mountain on the shore. He hesitated for a moment whether to turn back, and then, when the helmsman warned him to do so, he exclaimed, "Fortune favors the bold; try to reach Pomponianus." The latter was at Stabiae, separated by the whole width of the bay, for the sea there pours in upon a gently rounded and curving shore.

Although the danger was not yet close upon him,
it was none the less clearly seen, and it traveled quickly
as it came nearer, so Pomponianus had got his baggage
together on shipboard, and had determined upon flight,
and was waiting for the wind which was blowing on
shore to fall. My uncle sailed in with the wind fair
behind him, and embraced Pomponianus, who was in
a state of fright, comforting and cheering him at the
same time. Then in order to calm his friend's fears by
showing how composed he was himself, he ordered
the servants to carry him to the bath, and, after his
ablutions, he sat down and had dinner in the best of
spirits, or with that assumption of good spirits which is
quite as remarkable as the reality.

In the meantime broad sheets of flame, which
rose high in the air, were breaking out in a number of
places on Mount Vesuvius and lighting up the sky, and
the glare and brightness seemed all the more striking
owing to the darkness of the night. My uncle, in order
to allay the fear of his companions, kept declaring that
the country people in their terror had left their fires
burning, and that the conflagration they saw arose
from the blazing and empty villas. Then he betook
himself to rest and enjoyed a very deep sleep, for his
breathing, which, owing to his bulk, was rather heavy
and loud, was heard by those who were waiting at the
door of his chamber. But by this time the courtyard
leading to the room he occupied was so full of ashes
and pumice-stones mingled together, and covered to
such a depth, that if he had delayed any longer in the
bedchamber there would have been no means of escape.
So my uncle was aroused, and came out and joined
Pomponianus and the rest who had been keeping

watch. They held a consultation whether they should remain indoors or wander forth in the open; for the buildings were beginning to shake with the repeated and intensely severe shocks of earthquake, and seemed to be rocking to and fro as though they had been torn from their foundations. Outside again there was danger to be apprehended from the pumice-stones, though these were light and nearly burnt through, and thus, after weighing the two perils, the latter course was determined upon. With my uncle it was a choice of reasons which prevailed, with the rest a choice of fears.

They placed pillows on their heads and secured them with cloths, as a precaution against the falling bodies. Elsewhere the day had dawned by this time, but there it was still night, and the darkness was blacker and thicker than any ordinary night. This, however, they relieved as best they could by a number of torches and other kinds of lights. They decided to make their way to the shore, and to see from the nearest point whether the sea would enable them to put out, but it was still running high and contrary. A sheet was spread on the ground, and on this my uncle lay, and twice he called for a draft of cold water, which he drank. Then the flames, and the smell of sulphur which gave warning of them, scattered the others in flight and roused him. Leaning on two slaves, he rose to his feet and immediately fell down again, owing, as I think, to his breathing being obstructed by the thickness of the fumes and congestion of the stomach, that organ being naturally weak and narrow, and subject to inflammation. When daylight returned—two days after the last day he had seen—his body was found untouched, uninjured, and covered, dressed just as he had been in life. The corpse suggested a person asleep rather than a dead man.

Meanwhile my mother and I were at Misenum. But that is of no consequence for the purposes of history, nor indeed did you express a wish to be told of anything except of my uncle's death. So I will say no more, except to add that I have given you a full account both of the incidents which I myself witnessed and of those narrated to me immediately afterward, when, as a rule, one gets the truest account of what has happened. You will pick out what you think will answer your purpose best, for to write a letter is a different thing from writing a history, and to write to a friend is not like writing to all and sundry.

Farewell.

Voltaire to M. Tronchin, 24 November 1755

Voltaire was the most famous European of his day and a master of the art of letter writing in its golden age. His letters were often copied out for public distribution and read across the continent. Voltaire—real name François-Marie Arouet, born in 1694—was the polymathic French author of the satirical novel *Candide* and of poetry, history, and essays. He corresponded with monarchs like Frederick the Great and Catherine the Great while he amassed a huge fortune through financial speculation. *"Écrasez l'infâme!"* he often wrote—wipe out superstition, particularly with regard to religion. His wit was razor-sharp: "I disapprove of what you say, but I will defend to the death your right to say it."

Voltaire initially enjoyed the king's patronage, but soon

ran afoul of royal censorship and retired to live in splendor at
his chateau in Switzerland. His first great love was the clever
beauty the Marquise du Châtelet—a mother of three who was
also a philosopher and scientist—and then after her death, his
own young niece. On All Saints' Day 1755 an earthquake hit
Lisbon, killing over thirty thousand, a natural disaster that
shocked Europe. Voltaire wrote his *Poem on the Disaster of Lisbon* in response to the destruction. Here in a letter he considers
the meaning of such events in a way that seems just as appropriate today.

> This is indeed a cruel piece of natural philosophy!
> We shall find it difficult to discover how the laws of
> movement operate in such fearful disasters in the best
> of all possible worlds—where a hundred thousand
> ants, our neighbors, are crushed in a second on our
> ant-heaps, half dying undoubtedly in inexpressible
> agonies, beneath débris from which it was impossible
> to extricate them, families all over Europe reduced to
> beggary, and the fortunes of a hundred merchants—
> Swiss, like yourself—swallowed up in the ruins of
> Lisbon. What a game of chance human life is! What
> will the preachers say—especially if the Palace of
> the Inquisition is left standing! I flatter myself that
> those reverend fathers, the Inquisitors, will have been
> crushed just like other people. That ought to teach men
> not to persecute men: for, while a few sanctimonious
> humbugs are burning a few fanatics, the earth opens
> and swallows up all alike. I believe it is our mountains
> which save us from earthquakes.

Friendship

Captain A. D. Chater to his mother, Christmas 1914

Captain A.D. "Dougan" Chater, of the 2nd Battalion Gordon Highlanders, writes this letter home in the hope that the chivalry, decency, and friendship shown by both sides in the first Christmas of conflict will overcome the duty to fight and kill. When the Great War started in August 1914, most people presumed it would be over by Christmas. It wasn't, and instead the war deteriorated into the slaughter of trench warfare. But here Chater describes the "extraordinary sights" of the Christmas Truce of that first year of war. He does not mention the football games that took place between the English and the Germans in other sectors of the Front. Chater was later wounded at the Battle of Neuve Chapelle in March 1915, but survived, married his girlfriend Joy in 1916, and lived until 1974.

Dearest Mother,

I am writing this in the trenches in my "dug out"— with a wood fire going and plenty of straw. It is rather cozy although it is freezing hard and real Christmas weather.

I think I have seen one of the most extraordinary sights today that anyone has ever seen. About 10 o'clock this morning I was peeping over the parapet when I saw a German waving his arms and presently two of

them got out of their trenches and came toward ours.
We were just going to fire on them when we saw they
had no rifles so one of our men went out to meet them
and in about two minutes the ground between the two
lines of trenches was swarming with men and officers
of both sides, shaking hands and wishing each other
a happy Christmas. This continued for about half an
hour when most of our men were ordered back to the
trenches.

For the rest of the day nobody has fired a shot and
men have been wandering about at will on the top of
the parapet and carrying straw and fire wood about
in the open.

We have also had joint burial parties with a
service for some of the dead—some German and
some ours—who were lying out between the lines.
Some of our officers were taking groups of British
and German soldiers. This extraordinary truce
has been quite impromptu. There was no previous
arrangement and of course it had been decided that
there was not to be any cessation of hostilities.
I went out myself and shook hands with several of
their officers and men. From what I gathered most
of them would be as glad to get home again as we
should. We have had our pipes playing all day and
everyone has been wandering about in the open
unmolested but not of course as far as the enemy lines.
The truce will probably go on until someone is foolish
enough to let off his rifle. We nearly messed it up this
afternoon, by one of our fellows letting off his rifle
skywards by mistake but they did not seem to notice it
so it did not matter. I have been taking advantage of the
truce to improve my "dug out" which I share with D

M Bain, the Scotch rugger international—an excellent fellow.

We put on a proper roof this morning and now we have got a tiled fire place and brushwood and straw on the floor. We leave the trenches tomorrow and I shan't be sorry as it is much too cold to be pleasant at nights.

27th. I am writing this back in billets—the same business continues as yesterday and we had another parley with the Germans in the middle. We exchanged cigarettes and autographs and some more people took photos.

I don't know how long it will go on for—I believe it was supposed to stop yesterday but we can hear no firing going on along the front today except a little distant shelling.

We are, at any rate, having another truce on New Year's Day as the Germans want to see how the photos come out! Yesterday was lovely in the morning and I went for several quite long walks about the lines. It is difficult to realize what that means but of course in the ordinary way there is not a sign of life above ground and everyone who puts his head up gets shot at.

It is really very extraordinary that this sort of thing should happen in a war in which there is so much bitterness and ill feeling. The Germans in the front of the line are certainly sportsmen if they are nothing else. Of course I don't suppose it has happened everywhere along the line although I think that indiscriminate fighting has more or less stopped in most places on Christmas Day. . . .

Your loving son,
Dougan

Mark Antony to Octavian (later Augustus), c.33 BC

When two friends rule the world, this is the letter they write when they fall out because one of them falls in love with an Egyptian queen.

The heir to the Roman dictator Julius Caesar was his teenage great-nephew Octavian. In 44 BC, Caesar was assassinated. Octavian came to Rome to seek vengeance, forming an alliance with his uncle's top henchman, Mark Antony. After destroying the assassins led by Brutus and Cassius, Octavian and Antony divide the Roman world, Octavian ruling Rome and the west while Antony governs the east from Antioch, including Syria and the client kingdom of Egypt. Antony marries Octavian's sister Octavia to cement their alliance.

Egypt, the richest surviving state in Antony's east, is ruled by Cleopatra, heir to the grandest royal dynasty of the ancient world, the Ptolemies, who were Greeks descended from one of Alexander the Great's generals. Now that the Mediterranean is dominated by Rome, she needs the favor of the strongman of Rome. Earlier, she had had an affair with Caesar himself, bearing him a son. Now, aged thirty, she meets the buff and virile soldier Antony, and they fall in love and have children. Together they rule the east with a mixture of Greek style and eastern ritual, promising kingdoms to their children as if it is Antony's personal empire. The Romans sneer at Antony for his showy decadence: Octavian encourages the idea that a Roman imperator under the control of an Oriental queen is effete, unmanly, un-Roman. Furious at Octavian's manipulations back in Rome, Antony fires this earthy letter to his ex-friend, mocking the hypocrisy of this well-known womanizer. But Octavian's lovers were Roman, and Antony, isolated in his eastern grandeur with the fascinating Cleopatra, fails to see how dangerous his situation is becoming: he has lost the support of Rome. The two move toward war: in 31 BC, Octavian defeats Antony and Cleopatra at sea, and the lovers commit suicide. Taking the name Augustus (meaning "Illustrious"), Octavian then becomes Rome's first emperor.

What has come over you? Do you object to me screwing Cleopatra? But we are married; and it's not even as if this is anything new—the affair started nine years ago. And what about you? Are you faithful to Livia Drusilla? My congratulations if when this letter arrives you have not been to bed with Tertullia or Terentilla or Rufilla or Salvia Titisenia—or all of them. Does it really matter so much where or with whom one gets it up?

Between Karl Marx and Friedrich Engels,
July 1862–November 1864

The letters between Karl Marx and Friedrich Engels are shockingly racist to modern ears, but they reveal some of the flaws at the heart of Marxism. Marx and his friend Engels were the creators of an ideology known as Marxism that changed the world. Both born in Prussian territory, Marx was the son of Jewish intellectuals while Engels's father was a wealthy industrialist, a cotton manufacturer. But both were fascinated, horrified, and inspired by the cruel inequalities of the capitalist system and the plight of the working class. When they met in 1844 in Paris, Engels, then working on *The Condition of the Working Class in England*, convinced Marx that the working class itself would be the engine for a future revolution. Moving between Brussels and Britain, the two cooperated in the creation of a secret revolutionary movement, the League of the Just, which became the Communist League, and wrote their seminal text, *The Communist Manifesto*, with its famed opening sentence: "The history of all hitherto existing society is the history of class struggles." In this and Marx's future work *Das Kapital,* the two argued that the capitalist exploitation of the working class would lead to a class struggle and ultimately a revolution by the oppressed proletariat as well as a new era of equality and communism in which the state, no longer necessary, would wither away.

Marx's and Engels's most exciting moments were during the feverish months of the 1848 revolutions, but when the revolutions were crushed, they retreated to Britain. Engels helped run his family companies and paid Marx's expenses. In their long correspondence, Marx called himself "the Moor" (for his swarthiness) while Engels was "the General." While Engels lived with two sisters, who in turn were his mistresses, Marx was married to a well-connected and long-suffering Prussian baroness, Jenny von Westphalen. Jenny, while living in increasing poverty in Soho and Primrose Hill in London, bore him seven children, four of whom died young. Meanwhile, Marx was having adulterous affairs with their housekeeper, Helene Demuth, with whom he had a son.

Engels was jovial, social, and pleasure-loving; Marx was brooding, selfish, and intolerant but also enjoyed gossip and dancing. Both men were wildly jealous of their fellow socialist, Ferdinand Lassalle, who was in many ways what they wished to be: a political star, bon vivant, brilliant showman, and brazen lover who founded his own organization and was supported financially by his mistress, Countess von Hatzfeldt. Lassalle was so charismatic and influential that the reactionary minister-president Otto von Bismarck consulted him secretly.

Lassalle recognized Marx's talent and originality, helping him to get his work published, but both Marx and Engels maliciously repaid the favor with an endless stream of racist epithets, from "stupid Yid" to "Jewboy" and the even more racist "nigger." The first letter quoted here reveals their weirdly anti-Semitic and racist analysis of Lassalle. Two years later, Lassalle embarked on an affair with a young woman engaged to a Wallachian prince whom he foolishly challenged to a duel. Lassalle was killed. Marx and Engels were astonished by the rise and fall of this flamboyant meteor—and above all by Engels's reflections on Lassalle's intellectual and sexual power are particularly striking: "she didn't want his beautiful mind but his Jewish cock."

Marx to Engels

LONDON, 30 JULY 1862

Dear Engels,

From the enclosed scraps you'll see up to a point how I am bothered. The landlord meanwhile has been pacified, he has to get £25. The piano man, who is paid in instalments for the piano, was to have received £6 on the last day of June, and is a very rude lout. I have tax demands for £6 in the house. That school muck of about £10 I have fortunately paid since I'm doing all I can to spare the children direct humiliation. I've paid the butcher £6 (and this was my total quarterly income from Presse!) but the blighter is pestering me again, not to mention the baker, the teagrocer, the greengrocer and whatever the names of those devils are.

That Jewish nigger Lassalle, who is fortunately leaving at the end of this week, has happily again lost 5,000 Taler in a mis-speculation. The blighter would sooner fling his money into the mud than lend it to a "friend," even if interest as well as capital were guaranteed him. At the same time he proceeds from the view that he has to live as a Jewish baron or baronized (probably by the Countess) Jew. Would you believe it that the blighter, who is aware of the business with America, etc., i.e. is aware of the crisis in which I find myself, had the impertinence to ask me if I wanted to hand one of my daughters over to the Hatzfeldt woman as "companion" and whether he himself should obtain for me Gerstenberg's [sic] protection! The fellow cost me a lot of time and, so the oaf suggested, since at the moment I had "no business" but was engaged merely on "theoretical work," I might just as well kill time with him! In order to observe a certain social propriety vis-à-vis the fellow my wife had to take anything that was not actually screwed down to the pawnshop!

If I weren't in this hideous position, and if the parvenu's slapping of his money-bag did not irritate me so, I would have been royally amused. Since I saw him a year ago he has become totally mad. His stay in Zurich (with Rüstow, Herwegh, etc.) and his subsequent journey, and finally his "Herr Julian Schmidt," etc., have completely gone to his head. He is now by general agreement not only the greatest scholar, the most profound thinker, the most inspired researcher, etc., but also Don Juan and a revolutionary Cardinal Richelieu. And with it that unceasing babbling in his squeaking falsetto voice, his unaesthetically demonstrative movement, his didactic tone! . . .

. . . Lasalle was most furious about me and wife for poking fun at his plans, poking fun at him as an "enlightened Bonapartist," etc. He screamed, raved,

jumped about and in the end utterly convinced himself
that I am too "abstract" to understand politics.

   . . . As I said, in different circumstances (and if
he had not got into the way of my work) the blighter
would have royally amused me.

   Add to this the immoderate beast-like eating and
the randy lust of this "idealist."

   It is now perfectly clear to me that, as testified
also by his cranial formation and hair growth, he is
descended from the negroes who joined Moses's exodus
from Egypt (unless his paternal mother or grandmother
was crossed with a nigger). Well, this combination
of Jewish and Germanic stock with the negroid base
substance is bound to yield a strange product. The
fellow's importunity is also nigger-like. . . .

                                               Yours, K. M.

LONDON, 2 SEPTEMBER 1864

Dear Frederick,
   Yesterday afternoon I received the letter from
Freiligrath copied below, from which you will see that
Lassalle was critically wounded in a duel in Geneva. I
went to see Freiligrath the same evening. But he had
not received any later telegrams. . . .

                                               Yours, K. M.

Engels to Marx

MANCHESTER, 4 SEPTEMBER 1864

Dear Moor,

Your telegram arrived yesterday, even before
I opened your letter since all kinds of business
immediately took up my time. You may as well imagine
the news surprised me. Whatever else Lassalle may
have been, as a person, as a literary man, as a scholar—
politically he was certainly one of the most significant
fellows in Germany. To us at present he was a very
uncertain friend, in future a fairly certain enemy, but
be that as it may—it does hit one hard to see Germany
finishing off all reasonably good people of the extremist
party. What jubilation will reign now among the
manufacturers and among those progressive pigs.
Lassalle after all was the only chap in Germany itself of
whom they were afraid.

But what a strange way to lose one's life: to fall
seriously in love with the daughter of a Bavarian
envoy—that would-be Don Juan—to want to marry
her, to clash with a retired rival, who moreover is a
Wallachian cheat, and to be shot dead by him. That
could only happen to Lassalle, given his strange mixture
of frivolity and sentimentality, Jewishness and cavalier
posturing that was his and his alone. How could a
political man like him shoot it out with a Wallachian
adventurer! . . .

Yours, F. E.

Marx to Engels

LONDON, 7 SEPTEMBER 1864

Dear Frederick,

Lassalle's disaster has been damnably on my mind these days. When all is said and done, he was one of the old stock and the enemy of our enemies. Besides, the thing came as such a surprise that it is hard to believe that such a boisterous, stirring, pushing person is now dead as a door-nail and has to keep utterly silent. As for the ostensible occasion for his death, you are quite right. It is another of the many tactless actions he has committed in his life. With all that I am sorry that during the past few years our relationship was troubled, albeit through his fault. . . .

Yours, K. M.

Engels to Marx

MANCHESTER, 7 NOVEMBER 1864

Dear Moor,

. . . Evidently Lassalle's undoing was that he did not immediately fling Helene von Dönniges on to the bed in the guest-house and have a good go at her; she didn't want his beautiful mind but his Jewish cock. It's simply one more affair that could only have happened to Lassalle. That *he* forced the Wallachian to duel is doubly crazy. . . .

Yours, F. E.

Franklin D. Roosevelt to Winston Churchill,
11 September 1939

The first letter of the friendship that would hold the West.

On 3 September 1939, Britain declared war on Germany, which had invaded Poland. The Second World War had begun. Churchill returned to the cabinet as first lord of the Admiralty, the job he had held in 1914, the start of the First World War. A few days later, he received this letter from the US president Franklin Roosevelt who had served in a similar job—assistant secretary of the Navy, during the same war. They had met in passing twenty years earlier, and in 1933 when Roosevelt won the presidential election Churchill had sent him a copy of his biography of the Duke of Marlborough, but he had not acknowledged it. Now he does so—and opens up a secret channel with Churchill. Although Roosevelt mentions Prime Minister Neville Chamberlain in this letter, it is a formality since both men know how inept Chamberlain has been in appeasing Hitler. Roosevelt is betting that Churchill is the coming man. When he became prime minister eight months later, their alliance would be decisive.

My dear Churchill,

It is because you and I occupied similar positions in the [first] world war that I want you to know how glad I am that you are back again in the Admiralty. Your problems are, I realize, complicated by new factors, but the essential is not very different. What I want you and the Prime Minister to know is that I shall at all times welcome it if you will keep me in touch personally with anything you want me to know about. You can always send sealed letters through your pouch or my pouch.

I am glad you did the Marlborough volumes before this thing started—and I much enjoyed reading them. With my sincere regards,

Faithfully yours,
Franklin D. Roosevelt

Adolf Hitler to Benito Mussolini, 21 June 1941

A letter from Hitler to his closest friend in international affairs at the height of his power. It is written the night before he invades Soviet Russia, the hubristic act that ultimately led to the downfall of the Third Reich. Hitler had once admired Benito Mussolini, Fascist dictator of Italy since 1922, basing many of his tactics, even the creation of his own Nazi party, on Italian Fascism. But by 1941 Hitler saw him as a preposterous blowhard, while the Italian Duce regarded Hitler as a coarse and dangerous tyrant. But Hitler was now the senior partner. The letter is filled with half-truths: he has actually been planning the Russian invasion for many months (hiding it from Mussolini); and his swaggering delusions and brutal miscalculations are starkly revealed in the extraordinary way he boasts of a decision that would launch the most barbarous war in human history and cost the lives of over thirty million people. This is the way he sees the world when he believes no one can stop him.

21 JUNE 1941

Duce!
I am writing this letter to you at a moment when months of anxious deliberation and continuous nerve-

racking waiting are ending in the hardest decision of my life. I believe—after seeing the latest Russian situation map and after appraisal of numerous other reports—that I cannot take the responsibility for waiting longer, and above all, I believe that there is no other way of obviating this danger—unless it be further waiting, which, however, would necessarily lead to disaster in this or the next year at the latest.

The situation: England has lost this war. With the right of the drowning person, she grasps at every straw which, in her imagination, might serve as a sheet anchor. Nevertheless, some of her hopes are naturally not without a certain logic. England has thus far always conducted her wars with help from the Continent. The destruction of France—fact, the elimination of all west-European positions—directing the glances of the British warmongers continually to the place from which they tried to start the war: to Soviet Russia.

Both countries, Soviet Russia and England, are equally interested in a Europe fallen into ruin, rendered prostrate by a long war. Behind these two countries stands the North American Union goading them on and watchfully waiting. Since the liquidation of Poland, there is evident in Soviet Russia a consistent trend, which, even if cleverly and cautiously, is nevertheless reverting firmly to the old Bolshevist tendency to expansion of the Soviet State. The prolongation of the war necessary for this purpose is to be achieved by tying up German forces in the East, so that—particularly in the air—the German Command can no longer vouch for a large-scale attack in the West. I declared to you only recently, Duce, that it was precisely the success

of the experiment in Crete that demonstrated how
necessary it is to make use of every single airplane in
the much greater project against England. It may well
happen that in this decisive battle we would win with a
superiority of only a few squadrons. I shall not hesitate
a moment to undertake such a responsibility if, aside
from all other conditions, I at least possess the one
certainty that I will not then suddenly be attacked or
even threatened from the East. The concentration of
Russian forces—I had General Jodl submit the most
recent map to your Attaché here, General Maras—is
tremendous. Really, all available Russian forces are
at our border. Moreover, since the approach of warm
weather, work has been proceeding on numerous
defenses. If circumstances should give me cause to
employ the German air force against England, there
is a danger that Russia will then begin its strategy of
extortion in the South and North, to which I would
have to yield in silence, simply from a feeling of air
inferiority. It would, above all, not then be possible
for me without adequate support from an air force,
to attack the Russian fortifications with the divisions
stationed in the East. If I do not wish to expose myself
to this danger, then perhaps the whole year of 1941
will go by without any change in the general situation.
On the contrary. England will be all the less ready for
peace, for it will be able to pin its hopes on the Russian
partner. Indeed, this hope must naturally even grow
with the progress in preparedness of the Russian
armed forces. And behind this is the mass delivery
of war material from America which they hope to get
in 1942.

Aside from this, Duce, it is not even certain whether I shall have this time, for with so gigantic a concentration of forces on both sides—for I also was compelled to place more and more armored units on the eastern border, also to call Finland's and Romania's attention to the danger—there is the possibility that the shooting will start spontaneously at any moment. A withdrawal on my part would, however, entail a serious loss of prestige for us. This would be particularly unpleasant in its possible effect on Japan. I have, therefore, after constantly racking my brains, finally reached the decision to cut the noose before it can be drawn tight. I believe, Duce, that I am hereby rendering probably the best possible service to our joint conduct of the war this year. For my overall view is now as follows:

1. France is, as ever, not to be trusted. Absolute surety that North Africa will not suddenly desert does not exist.

2. North Africa itself, insofar as your colonies, Duce, are concerned, is probably out of danger until autumn. I assume that the British, in their last attack, wanted to relieve Tobruk. I do not believe they will soon be in a position to repeat this.

3. Spain is irresolute and—I am afraid—will take sides only when the outcome of the war is decided.

4. In Syria, French resistance can hardly be maintained permanently either with or without our help.

5. An attack on Egypt before autumn is out of the question altogether. I consider it necessary, however, taking into account the whole situation, to give thought to the development of an operational unit

in Tripoli itself which can, if necessary, also be launched against the West. Of course, Duce, the strictest silence must be maintained with regard to these ideas, for otherwise we cannot expect France to continue to grant permission to use its ports for the transportation of arms and munitions.

6. Whether or not America enters the war is a matter of indifference, inasmuch as she supports our opponent with all the power she is able to mobilize.

7. The situation in England itself is bad; the provision of food and raw materials is growing steadily more difficult. The martial spirit to make war, after all, lives only on hopes. These hopes are based solely on two assumptions: Russia and America. We have no chance of eliminating America. But it does lie in our power to exclude Russia. The elimination of Russia means, at the same time, a tremendous relief for Japan in East Asia, and thereby the possibility of a much stronger threat to American activities through Japanese intervention.

I have decided under these circumstances as I already mentioned, to put an end to the hypocritical performance in the Kremlin. I assume, that is to say, I am convinced, that Finland, and likewise Romania, will forthwith take part in this conflict, which will ultimately free Europe, for the future also, of a great danger. General Maras informed us that you, Duce, wish also to make available at least one corps. If you have that intention, Duce—which I naturally accept with a heart filled with gratitude—the time for carrying it out will still be sufficiently long, for in this immense theatre of war the troops cannot be assembled at all

points at the same time anyway. You, Duce, can give
the decisive aid, however, by strengthening your forces
in North Africa, also, if possible, looking from Tripoli
toward the West, by proceeding further to build up
a group which, though it be small at first, can march
into France in case of a French violation of the treaty;
and finally, by carrying the air war and, so far as it is
possible, the submarine war, in intensified degree, into
the Mediterranean.

So far as the security of the territories in the West
is concerned, from Norway to and including France,
we are strong enough there—so far as army troops are
concerned—to meet any eventuality with lightning
speed. So far as air war on England is concerned, we
shall, for a time remain on the defensive,—but this does
not mean that we might be incapable of countering
British attacks on Germany; on the contrary, we shall,
if necessary, be in a position to start ruthless bombing
attacks on British home territory. Our fighter defense,
too, will be adequate. It consists of the best squadrons
that we have.

As far as the war in the East is concerned, Duce,
it will surely be difficult, but I do not entertain a
second's doubt as to its great success. I hope, above
all, that it will then be possible for us to secure a
common food-supply base in the Ukraine for some
time to come, which will furnish us such additional
supplies as we may need in the future. I may state at
this point, however, that, as far as we can tell now, this
year's German harvest promises to be a very good one.
It is conceivable that Russia will try to destroy the
Romanian oil region. We have built up a defense that
will—or so I think—prevent the worst. Moreover, it is

the duty of our armies to eliminate this threat as rapidly as possible.

I waited until this moment, Duce, to send you this information, it is because the final decision itself will not be made until 7 o'clock tonight. I earnestly beg you, therefore, to refrain, above all, from making any explanation to your Ambassador at Moscow, for there is no absolute guarantee that our coded reports cannot be decoded. I, too, shall wait until the last moment to have my own Ambassador informed of the decisions reached.

The material that I now contemplate publishing gradually, is so exhaustive that the world will have more occasion to wonder at our forbearance than at our decision, except for that part of the world which opposes us on principle and for which, therefore, arguments are of use.

Whatever may now come, Duce, our situation cannot become worse as a result of this step; it can only improve. Even if I should be obliged at the end of this year to leave 60 or 70 divisions in Russia, that is only a fraction of the forces that I am now continually using on the eastern front. Should England nevertheless not draw any conclusions from the hard facts that present themselves, then we can, with our rear secured, apply ourselves with increased strength to the dispatching of our opponent. I can promise you, Duce, that what lies in our German power, will be done.

Any desires, suggestions, and assistance of which you, Duce, wish to inform me in the contingency before us, I would request that you either communicate to me personally or have them agreed upon directly by our military authorities.

In conclusion, let me say one more thing, Duce. Since I struggled through to this decision, I again feel spiritually free. The partnership with the Soviet Union, in spite of the complete sincerity of the efforts to bring about a final conciliation, was nevertheless often very irksome to me, for in some way or other it seemed to me to be a break with my whole origin, my concepts, and my former obligations. I am happy now to be relieved of these mental agonies.

With hearty and comradely greetings,
Your ADOLF HITLER

Between Prince Potemkin and Catherine the Great, c.1774

How to settle a row—by letter (or email). Catherine the Great and Prince Potemkin, her brilliant lover and minister, were wildly in love with each other, but he was restless at being at her beck and call: he wanted to be a chief minister, a commander, an empire builder.

After an argument, he calmly apologizes for his tempestuous nature and then on the same piece of paper she answers his complaints in this double letter, concluding "End of quarrel." It is not unlike an email thread. But even this civilized negotiation did not solve the problem, until she secretly married him and agreed that they would continue ruling like husband and wife—except both would be allowed their own, younger, lovers. The strange arrangement worked, and they ruled Russia together with great success for almost twenty years, ending only with Potemkin's death in 1791. She survived another five years but she never got over the prince: "There'll never be another Potemkin," she often said.

Potemkin	Catherine
Let me my love say this	I allow it.
Which will, I hope, end our argument.	The sooner the better.
Don't be surprised I am Disturbed by our love.	Don't be disturbed.
Not only have you showered me With good deeds, You have placed me in your Heart. I want to be There alone, and above everyone else	You are there firmly & strongly & will remain there.
Because no one has ever loved you so much	I see it and believe it.
And I have been made by your hands	Happy to do so.
That you should be happy in being good To me;	It will be my greatest pleasure.
That you should find rest from the Great labors arising from your high Station in thinking of my comfort.	Of course.
Amen.	Give rest to our thoughts and let our feelings act freely. They are most tender and will find the best way. End of quarrel. Amen.

Folly

Georg von Hülsen to Emil von Görtz, 1892

The courtiers of Kaiser Wilhelm II, the leader of the German empire, tried hard, year after year, to provide the sort of crass entertainment their monarch craved. During his long reign—1888 to 1918—his political and diplomatic antics not only appalled his own officials and ministers, but also alarmed the chancelleries of Europe, thereby raising the tensions that led to the First World War.

Bombastic, brutish, and boastful; narcissistic and vain; nationalistic, inconsistent, and impulsive; obsessed with power and claiming credit for everything while operating under the burdens of a mountainous ego and matching inferiority complex, Wilhelm is in some ways a familiar modern character. He also possessed an extremely childish sense of humor. He delighted in cutting his generals' braces off with his penknife, or chasing old colonels to bed, or rolling them downhill. Cross-dressing, sausages, and bare bottoms were also royal favorites. As we see in this extract from a letter sent before a hunt in 1892, close friend Count "Em" von Görtz knows exactly what pranks will please the kaiser, planning it with courtier Georg von Hülsen. Their games could go wrong. In 1908, Dietrich von Hülsen, Georg's brother, danced for the kaiser in full ballerina costume, complete with tutu, feather boa, and satin pumps—until he fell down dead of a heart attack. Such were the entertainments of the most powerful man in the world: "I can already see H.M. [His Majesty] laughing . . ."

> You must be paraded by me as a circus poodle!—That will "hit" like nothing else. Just think: behind shaved [tights], in front long bangs out of black or white wool, at the back under a genuine poodle tail a marked rectal opening and, when you beg, in front a fig-leaf. Just think how wonderful when you bark, howl to music, shoot off a pistol or do other tricks. It is simply splendid!! . . . In my mind's eye I can already see H.M. [His Majesty] laughing with us. . . . I am applying myself with real relish to this "work" in order to forget that my beloved sister—the dearest thing I have on earth—is at this moment dying in Breslau. . . . I feel like the clown in [Ludwig] Knaus's picture "Behind the Scenes." No matter!—H.M. shall be satisfied!

The Marquis de Sade "to the stupid villains who torment me," 1783

A letter of sadism. The philosopher, libertine, and sexual deviant, Donatien, Marquis de Sade spent nearly half of his life in prisons or mental asylums, accused of sodomy and perversion. As a boy, it was a schoolmaster's thrashing that ignited a fascination with pain and pleasure—and the connection between the two. Abandoned by his aristocratic family, his playful and cruel whims were indulged by servants. He served in the army while he embarked on a spree of seductions, beatings, torments, and sodomy with women and men of all ages, some of them distastefully young. Promoted to colonel during the Seven Years' War, he married a magistrate's daughter Renée-Pélagie de Montreuil, with whom he had three children. Their marriage soon failed, and when he was faced with a blizzard of denunciations for perversion that almost led to his execution, his mother-in-law, Mme. de Montreuil, won him some protection from the law by procuring a *lettre de cachet,* a royal letter that allowed de Sade to be confined indefinitely without trial.

In prison de Sade wrote his brilliant but demented and obscene novels, such as *Justine,* which were as maniacally brazen and violently ingenuous as his orgies. Confined to the Château de Vincennes between 1777 and 1784, de Sade amuses himself by writing this vicious letter to his tormentors, especially "the strumpet," his mother-in-law, for whom he devises sadistic punishments. When the Revolution came, de Sade was in the Bastille writing *120 Days of Sodom* and encouraged the crowd to attack the fortress, but he was removed to a lunatic asylum before it fell to the revolutionaries. Nonetheless he was liberated and joined the Revolution, serving as a high official while enjoying his freedoms until he opposed Robespierre's Terror, which led to his arrest. He was lucky not to be guillotined. Napoleon Bonaparte returned him to the asylum, and while there he seduced the fourteen-year-old daughter of an employee. He died in 1814.

Vincennes,

Vile minions of the tunny-fish vendors of Aix, low and infamous servants of torturers, invent then for my torment tortures from which at least some good may result. What is the effect of the inaction in which your spiritual purblindness keeps me except to curse and lacerate the unworthy procuress who so meanly contrived to sell me to you? Since I can neither read nor write any longer, this is the hundred and eleventh torture which I am inventing for her. This morning as I suffered I saw her, the strumpet, I saw her flayed alive, dragged over thistles and then thrown into a barrel of vinegar. And I said to her:

Execrable creature that is for selling your son-in-law to the torturers!

Take that, you procuress, for hiring out your two daughters!

Take that for having ruined and dishonored your son-in-law!

Take that for making him hate the children for whose sake supposedly you sacrifice him!

Take that for having wrecked the best years of his life when it rested with you alone to help him after his sentence!

Take that for having preferred the vile and detestable offspring of your daughter to him!

Take that for all the wickedness with which you overwhelmed him for thirteen years, to make him pay for your stupidities!

And I increased her tortures, and insulted her in her pain and forgot mine.

My pen falls from my hand. I must suffer.

Adieu, torturers, I must curse you.

Between Empress Alexandra and Nicholas II, 1916

A wife writes to her beloved husband at the front during the First World War, in quaint upper-class English full of nick-names like Agooweeone (him) and Wify and Sunny (her). But this is no ordinary couple, and it is a letter that shows why Russia is just weeks from the revolution. This is Tsarina Alexandra in the country's capital, Petrograd, writing to her husband, Nicholas II, who is at military headquarters. She urges Nicholas to be "the master," like Peter the Great and Ivan the Terrible before him. Her advice is backed by the divine authority of "our Friend" Rasputin, whom she sees as the successor of the couple's earlier healer, a charlatan "doctor" named Monsieur Philippe. Obsessed with autocracy, halting democracy, and judging every political or military decision by whether it was good or bad for Rasputin, she is a catastrophic influence, aggressively proposing political appointments like her candidate for interior minister, Alexander Protopopov, a half-mad, cocaine-addicted syphilitic. She boasts that she is the most powerful woman in Russia since Catherine the Great. Her only redeeming feature is her devotion to her family and "Nicky" himself, whose caresses she longs for—as he does hers.

Alexandra to Nicholas, 14 December 1916

7 of frost and thick snow. Scarcely slept this night again, remaining till luncheon in bed as all aches still and have a slight chill. Such loving thanks for your dear letter.

Be Peter the Great, Ivan the Terrible, Emperor Paul—crush them all under you—now don't you laugh, naughty one.

I really cannot understand. I am but a woman, but my soul and brain tell me it would be the saving of Russia—they sin far worse than anything the Sukhomlinovs ever did. Forbid Brusilov etc. when they come to touch any political subjects, fool, who wants responsible cabinet.

Remember even M. Philippe said one dare not give

constitution, as it would be your and Russia's ruin, and all true Russians say the same.

Months ago I told [Premier] Sturmer about Shvedov to be a member of Council of the Empire to have them and good Maklokov in they will stand bravely for us. I know I worry you—ah, would I not far, far rather only write letters of love, tenderness and caresses of which my heart is so full—but my duty as wife and mother and Russia's mother obliges me to say all to you—blessed by our Friend.

Sweetheart, sunshine of my life, if in battle you had to meet the enemy, you would never waver and go forth like a lion—be it now in the battle against the small handful of brutes and republicans.

Be the Master, and all will bow down to you. Do you think I should fear, ah no—today I have had an officer cleared out from [their daughters] Maria's and Anastasia's hospital, because he allowed himself to mock at our journey, pretending Protopopov brought the people to receive us so well; the Doctors who heard it raged—you see Sunny in her small things is energetic and in big ones as much as you wish—we have been placed by God on a throne and we must keep it firm and give it over to our son untouched—if you keep that in mind you will remember to be the Sovereign—and how much easier for an autocratic sovereign than one who has sworn the Constitution.

Beloved One, listen to me, yes, you know your old true girly. "Do not fear," the old woman said and therefore I write without fear to me agooweeone. Now the girlies want their tea, they came frozen back from their drive—I kiss you and hold you tightly clasped to my breast, caress you, love you, long for you, can't sleep without you—bless you.

Ever your very Own
Wify

Nicholas's replies to Alexandra are equally a mix of misguided arrogance and intimate sentimentality. In this earlier letter he dreams of making love to her again—using the nickname "Boysy" for his sex: in her letters she calls hers "Lady." His loathing of Miechen, wife of his cousin Vladimir, reveals the growing feud with the rest of the Romanov family.

Nicholas to Alexandra, 16 June 1916

My own darling Wify,
    Today the messenger is a little late, probably
on account of new movements of troops fr north
to south. I send you a telegram which [their son,
Tsarevich] Aleksei got fr his regiment. Again good
news thank God fr Lechitsky! Yesterday his army
made 221 officers & 10,200 men prisoners! So many
new hands working in our fields & manufact[ories].
Miechen [Grand Duchess Maria Pavlovna] wrote me
a cold letter asking me why I have not approved the
polozhenie [Regulation]? I sent it through Alekseev to
the Verkh. Soviet. Perhaps you will let Ilin [president
of the Russian Red Cross] know that they are to look
at it though [sic] & send me their opinion. She is
really insufferable—if I have time, I shall answer her
sharply.—We have finished lunch & on coming up to
my room I found your dear letter No. 520. . . . How

I miss your sweet kisses! Yes, beloved One, you know how to give them! Oh, how naughtily! Boysy hops from remembrances. It is very hot & now a few drops of rain fell out of an isolated cloud. I hope to bathe in the river higher up while Aleksei runs about with naked legs. Did he describe to you how the small peasant boys play all sorts of games before us? Now, my precious Darling, I must end. God bless you & the girlies.

With many fond kisses ever your own <u>Nicky</u>.

Decency

Maria Theresa to Marie Antoinette, 30 July 1775

No child enjoys a strict telling-off from their mother, especially on the subjects of manners and morality. Here Empress Maria Theresa scolds her daughter Marie Antoinette, queen of France, for her high-handed rudeness to diplomats and ministers and for running around with flirtatious flatterers while ignoring her dull, weak husband, King Louis XVI. The mother is fifty-eight, the daughter nineteen. Maria Theresa has struggled through incessant wars to keep her vast empire together since she inherited it at the age of twenty-three. Then, thirty years later, in 1756, she has pulled a diplomatic coup by marrying her pretty daughter to the king of France. It is clear that the mother glimpses something so dangerous in her daughter that she foresees catastrophe. Maria Theresa would die in 1780; she never saw the "misfortune" she had feared—the French Revolution and the execution of her daughter.

Madame my dear daughter

I cannot hide from you that a letter you sent to [Minister] Rosenberg upset me most dreadfully. What style! What frivolity! Where is the good and generous heart of the Archduchess Antoinette? I see only intrigue, vulgar spite, delight in mockery and persecution. An intrigue which would do very well for

a Pompadour or a Dubarry, but never for a queen, a
great princess, still less a princess kindly and good of
the house of Lorraine and Austria. All the winter long
I have trembled at the thought of your too easy success
and the flatterers surrounding you, while you have
thrown yourself into a life of pleasure and preposterous
display. This chasing from pleasure to pleasure without
the king, and knowing that he takes no joy in it and
only goes with you or lets you do what you want out of
sheer good nature, has made me write before to express
my fears. I see now from this letter that these were all
too well justified. . . .

Your luck can all too easily change, and by your own
fault you may well find yourself plunged into deepest
misery. That is the result of your terrible dissipation
which prevents your being assiduous about anything
serious. What have you read? And after that you dare
to opine on the greatest State matters, on the choice
of ministers? What does the Abbé do? And Mercy?
You dislike them because of behaving like low flatterers
they want you to be happy and do not take advantage
of your weaknesses. One day you will recognize the
truth of this, but then it will be too late. I hope I shall
not survive until misfortune overtakes you, and I pray
to God to end my days quickly, since I am no longer
of any use to you, and I could not bear to lose my dear
child or see her unhappy, whom I shall love tenderly
until I die.

Mahatma Gandhi to Adolf Hitler, 24 December 1940

This letter is the ultimate clash of seraphic decency and diabolical evil. At the end of 1940, with the Nazi empire at its height, Europe conquered, Germany apparently invincible, Hitler receives a letter from his diametric opposite, Mahatma Gandhi, who is actively involved in attempting to eject the British from India. Gandhi campaigned against any Indian participation in the war, arguing that his country could not be involved in a conflict over freedom when such a right was denied to India itself. (Nonetheless, two and a half million of his countrymen joined the Allied forces.)

The seventy-one-year-old Indian activist had tried in 1939 to counsel Hitler against war and now appeals to the Führer's better nature by reminding him of his own struggles against British imperialism. He writes from his ashram in Sevagram in Maharashtra, where he lives with his wife and their four children. The letter is as futile as it is admirable. Hitler never replies, going on to perpetrate the Holocaust, invade Russia, and commit suicide in the ruins of Berlin. Gandhi's campaign was successful, leading the British to grant India (and Pakistan) independence. Soon afterward, Gandhi was assassinated by a fanatical Hindu gunman.

DECEMBER 24, 1940

DEAR FRIEND,

That I address you as a friend is no formality. I own no foes. My business in life has been for the past 33 years to enlist the friendship of the whole of humanity by befriending mankind, irrespective of race, color or creed.

I hope you will have the time and desire to
know how a good portion of humanity who have
been living under the influence of that doctrine
of universal friendship view your action. We have
no doubt about your bravery or devotion to your
fatherland, nor do we believe that you are the monster
described by your opponents. But your own writings
and pronouncements and those of your friends and
admirers leave no room for doubt that many of your
acts are monstrous and unbecoming of human dignity,
especially in the estimation of men like me who believe
in universal friendliness. Such are your humiliation of
Czechoslovakia, the rape of Poland and the swallowing
of Denmark. I am aware that your view of life regards
such spoliations as virtuous acts. But we have been
taught from childhood to regard them as acts degrading
humanity. Hence we cannot possibly wish success to
your arms.

But ours is a unique position. We resist British
Imperialism no less than Nazism. If there is a
difference, it is in degree. One-fifth of the human race
has been brought under the British heel by means that
will not bear scrutiny. Our resistance to it does not
mean harm to the British people. We seek to convert
them, not to defeat them on the battlefield. Ours is an
unarmed revolt against the British rule. But whether
we convert them or not, we are determined to make
their rule impossible by non-violent non-co-operation.
It is a method in its nature indefensible. It is based on
the knowledge that no spoliator can compass his end
without a certain degree of co-operation, willing or
compulsory, of the victim. Our rulers may have our land
and bodies but not our souls. . . .

We know what the British heel means for us and
the non-European races of the world. But we would
never wish to end the British rule with German aid. We
have found in non-violence a force which, if organized,
can without doubt match itself against a combination
of all the most violent forces in the world. In non-
violent technique, as I have said, there is no such thing
as defeat. It is all "do or die" without killing or hurting.
It can be used practically without money and obviously
without the aid of science or destruction which you
have brought to such perfection. It is a marvel to me
that you do not see that it is nobody's monopoly. If not
the British, some other power will certainly improve
upon your method and beat you with your own weapon.
You are leaving no legacy to your people of which they
would feel proud. They cannot take pride in a recital
of cruel deed, however skilfully planned. I, therefore,
appeal to you in the name of humanity to stop the
war. . . .

You know that not long ago I made an appeal to
every Briton to accept my method of non-violent
resistance. I did it because the British know me as a
friend though a rebel. I am a stranger to you and your
people. I have not the courage to make to you the
appeal I made to every Briton. Not that it would not
apply to you with the same force as to the British. But
my present proposal is much simpler because much
more practical and familiar.

During this season when the hearts of the peoples
of Europe yearn for peace, we have suspended even
our own peaceful struggle. Is it too much to ask you
to make an effort for peace during a time which may
mean nothing to you personally but which must mean

much to the millions of Europeans whose dumb cry
for peace I hear, for my ears are attended to hearing the
dumb millions?

I am,
Your sincere friend,
M. K. GANDHI

Abraham Lincoln to Ulysses S. Grant, 13 July 1863

Here President Abraham Lincoln congratulates General Grant
wholeheartedly for an important victory during the American Civil War—the capture of Vicksburg, Mississippi—and,
remarkably, apologizes for getting it completely wrong himself.
A masterful letter writer, Lincoln is famed for his clarity of language, whether political or personal. In a letter of 22 August
1862 he states his real priorities in the conflict: "I would save the
Union. I would save it the shortest way. . . . What I do about
slavery and the colored race I do because I believe it helps save
the Union. . . ."

But he also had a sense of fun: when an eleven-year-old girl
named Grace Bedell wrote to advise him to grow more presidential whiskers, Lincoln replied on 19 October 1860: "My dear
little Miss. . . . As for whiskers, having never worn any, do you
not think people would call it a piece of silly affectation if I were
to begin now? Your very sincere well wisher A. Lincoln."

However, this letter is significant strategically and because
of what it reveals about Lincoln's character. It means he has
finally found a victorious general: he promoted Grant to commanding general and Grant went on to be elected president. It
also highlights Lincoln's magnanimity and his confidence in his

own gifts. Such humility is rare among bosses of all kinds but especially among politicians.

> My dear General
> I do not remember that you and I ever met personally. I write this now as a grateful acknowledgment for the almost inestimable service you have done the country. I wish to say a word further. When you first reached the vicinity of Vicksburg, I thought you should do, what you finally did—march the troops across the neck, run the batteries with the transports, and thus go below; and I never had any faith, except a general hope that you knew better than I, that the Yazoo Pass expedition, and the like, could succeed. When you got below, and took Port-Gibson, Grand Gulf, and vicinity, I thought you should go down the river and join Gen. Banks; and when you turned Northward East of the Big Black, I feared it was a mistake. I now wish to make the personal acknowledgment that you were right, and I was wrong.
>
> *Yours very truly*
> A. Lincoln

John Profumo to Harold Macmillan, 5 June 1963

There is the sin, and there is the cover-up. Often the cover-up is worse. This letter of truth and confession ends an era. In 1961 John Profumo, secretary of state for war in Harold Macmillan's government, admired a beautiful model and demi-mondaine, Christine Keeler, bathing in the pool at Cliveden, the country house of Viscount Astor—and began an affair with her. At the same time she was having an affair with a KGB spy, Soviet naval attaché, Yevgeni Ivanov. Profumo, who was married, denied any "impropriety" to the prime minister and Parliament. But when the truth was exposed he was forced to write this letter to Macmillan. The "Profumo affair" fatally damages not just the Conservative government but also the old-fashioned public-school Establishment. Macmillan retires, Labour wins the next election, and Profumo devotes the rest of his life to charity.

Dear Prime Minister,

You will recollect that on 22 March, following certain allegations made in Parliament, I made a personal statement. At the time the rumor had charged me with assisting in the disappearance of a witness and with being involved in some possible breach of security.

So serious were these charges that I allowed myself to think that my personal association with that witness, which had also been the subject of rumor, was by comparison of minor importance only. In my statement I said there had been no impropriety in this association. To my very deep regret I have to admit that this was not true, and that I misled you and my colleagues and the House.

I ask you to understand that I did this to protect, as I thought, my wife and family, who were misled, as were my professional advisers.

I have come to realize that, by this deception, I have been guilty of a grave misdemeanor and despite the fact that there is no truth whatsoever in the other charges, I cannot remain a member of your Administration, nor of the House of Commons.

I cannot tell you of my deep remorse for the embarrassment I have caused you, to my colleagues in the Government, to my constituents, and to the Party which I have served for the past twenty-five years.

Yours sincerely,
Jack Profumo

Jacqueline Kennedy to Nikita Khrushchev, 1 December 1963

Chivalry in despair is the spirit of this letter written by Jackie Kennedy on one of her last nights in the White House, a week after the assassination of her husband, John F. Kennedy. The president and his adversary, the Soviet premier Nikita Khrushchev, were opposites: Kennedy a handsome, cultured, millionaire Lothario, Khrushchev a warty, brutal Communist peasant. They had had bruising negotiations—and only narrowly avoided launching the world into nuclear war. There were many in the CIA who feared the Russians might have played a role in planning the assassination. Khrushchev, for his part, was terrified of being blamed for it. Perhaps the letter that follows is written to calm the Russian—it is certainly supremely elegant and touching in both its literary simplicity, presidential grandeur, and its theory of Big Men and Little Men.

Dear Mr. Chairman President,

I would like to thank you for sending Mr. Mikoyan as your representative to my husband's funeral. He looked so upset when he came through the line, and I was very moved.

I tried to give him a message for you that day—but

as it was such a terrible day for me, I do not know if my words came out as I meant them to.

So now, on one of the last nights I will spend in the White House, in one of the last letters I will write on this paper in the White House, I would like to write you my message.

I send it only because I know how much my husband cared about peace, and how the relation between you and him was central to this care in his mind. He used to quote your words in some of his speeches—"in the next war the survivors will envy the dead."

You and he were adversaries, but you were allied in a determination that the world should not be blown up. You respected each other and could deal with each other. I know that President Johnson will make every effort to establish the same relationship with you.

The danger which troubled my husband was that war might be started not so much by the big men as by the little ones.

While big men know the needs for self-control and restraint—little men are sometimes moved more by fear and pride. If only in the future the big men can continue to make the little ones sit down and talk, before they start to fight.

I know that President Johnson will continue the policy in which my husband so deeply believed— a policy of control and restraint—and he will need your help.

I send this letter because I know so deeply of the importance of the relationship which existed between you and my husband, and also because of your kindness, and that of Mrs. Khrushchev in Vienna.

I read that she had tears in her eyes when she left the American Embassy in Moscow, after signing the book of mourning. Please thank her for that.

Sincerely,
Jacqueline Kennedy

Babur to his son Humayun, 11 January 1529

This is a letter of tolerance. Babur, born in 1483, was a prince descended from greatness, from the conqueror Tamurlane, in a family that had lost its glory. But almost single-handedly he restored its power, conquered the vastness of India, and founded his own dynasty known as the Mughals. In the famous memoirs *The Baburnama,* Babur writes of battles and polo matches, feasts and poetry, but he also knew how to rule the complex multi-religious society of India. Here, aged forty-five, shortly before his death, Emperor Babur gives advice to his son that is relevant today not just in India but also in the wider Islamic world.

Oh my son! The realm of Hindustan is full of diverse creeds. Praise be to God, the Righteous, the Glorious, the Highest, that He hath granted unto thee the Empire of it. It is but proper that you, with heart cleansed of all religious bigotry, should dispense justice according to the tenets of each community. And in particular refrain from the sacrifice of cow, for that way lies the conquest of the hearts of the people of Hindustan; and the subjects of the realm will, through royal favor, be devoted to thee. And the temples and abodes of worship of every community under Imperial sway, you should not damage. Dispense justice so that the sovereign may be happy with the subjects and likewise the subjects with their sovereign. The progress of Islam is better by the sword of kindness, not by the sword of oppression.

Ignore the disputations of Shias and Sunnis; for therein is the weakness of Islam. And bring together the subjects with different beliefs in the manner of the Four Elements, so that the body politic may be immune from the various ailments. And remember the deeds of Hazrat Taimur Sahib Qiran so that you may become mature in matters of Government. And on us is but the duty to advise.

Émile Zola to Félix Faure, 13 January 1898

This letter is a wonder of moral outrage. Zola's letter to the French president exposes the injustice and anti-Semitism of the French military that has already divided France in a vicious schism between two visions of the country: Catholic nationalism versus secular liberalism. Zola exposes the "shady creatures," shameful hypocrites, and despicable anti-Semites who have sentenced a totally innocent man to life on the hellish Devil's Island prison in French Guiana for treason—even when, two years later, they uncover the identity of the real German spy who really is guilty of betraying his country.

In December 1894, a young French captain from Alsace named Alfred Dreyfus, who happened to be Jewish, was convicted of selling French military secrets to German intelligence. The conviction was always highly suspect, but in 1896 French intelligence identified the real culprit as Major Ferdinand Esterhazy. Nonetheless, the French generals and politicians arranged for Esterhazy to be acquitted and covered up his guilt. As the brazen injustice and rampant racism divide France, the novelist Émile Zola, author of *Nana* and *Germinal*, decides he must speak out, publishing this letter exposing the men behind the framing of Dreyfus, the public campaign of anti-Semitism, and the cover-up.

Zola was tried for libel and had to flee to London, but the letter worked: the outcry forced the government to reopen the case. In 1899, broken after five years in captivity, Dreyfus returned for a second trial. Amazingly, he was convicted again and sentenced to ten years but was then pardoned and exonerated, his rank reinstated, dying in 1935 as a lieutenant-colonel. In 1902 Zola died of carbon-monoxide poisoning due to a blocked chimney: he may have been murdered for writing this letter. Its exposé of anti-Semitism is sadly relevant today.

Mr. President,

Would you allow me, grateful as I am for the kind reception you once extended to me, to show my concern about maintaining your well-deserved prestige and to point out that your star which, until now, has shone so brightly, risks being dimmed by the most shameful and indelible of stains?

Unscathed by vile slander, you have won the hearts of all. You are radiant in the patriotic glory of our country's alliance with Russia, you are about to preside over the solemn triumph of our World Fair, the jewel that crowns this great century of labor, truth, and freedom. But what filth this wretched Dreyfus affair has cast on your name—I wanted to say "reign." A court martial, under orders, has just dared to acquit a certain Esterhazy, a supreme insult to all truth and justice. And now the image of France is sullied by this filth, and history shall record that it was under your presidency that this crime against society was committed.

As they have dared, so shall I dare. Dare to tell the truth, as I have pledged to tell it, in full, since the normal channels of justice have failed to do so. My duty is to speak out; I do not wish to be an accomplice in this travesty. My nights would otherwise be haunted by the spectre of the innocent man, far away, suffering the most horrible of tortures for a crime he did not commit. . . .

But now we see Dreyfus appearing before the court martial. Behind the closed doors, the utmost secrecy is demanded. Had a traitor opened the border to the enemy and driven the Kaiser straight to Notre-Dame the measures of secrecy and silence could not have been more stringent. The public was astounded; rumors flew of the most horrible acts, the most monstrous deceptions, lies that were an affront to our history. The public, naturally, was taken in. No punishment could be too harsh. The people clamored for the traitor to be publicly stripped of his rank and demanded to see him writhing with remorse on his rock of infamy. Could these things be true, these unspeakable acts, these deeds so dangerous that they must be carefully hidden behind closed doors to keep Europe from going up in flames? No! They were nothing but the demented fabrications of Major du Paty de Clam, a cover-up of the most preposterous fantasies imaginable. To be convinced of this one need only read carefully the accusation as it was presented before the court martial.

How flimsy it is! The fact that someone could have been convicted on this charge is the ultimate iniquity. I defy decent men to read it without a stir of indignation in their hearts and a cry of revulsion, at the thought of the undeserved punishment being meted out there on Devil's Island. He knew several languages: a crime! He carried no compromising papers: a crime! He would occasionally visit his country of origin: a crime! He was hardworking, and strove to be well informed: a crime! He did not become confused: a crime! He became confused: a crime! And how childish the language is, how groundless the accusation! . . .

These, Sir, are the facts that explain how this miscarriage of justice came about; The evidence of Dreyfus's character, his affluence, the lack of motive and his continued affirmation of innocence combine to show that he is the victim of the lurid imagination of Major du Paty de Clam, the religious circles surrounding him, and the "dirty Jew" obsession that is the scourge of our time.

And now we come to the Esterhazy case. Three years have passed, many consciences remain profoundly troubled, become anxious, investigate, and wind up convinced that Dreyfus is innocent. . . .

As I have shown, the Dreyfus case was a matter internal to the War Office: an officer of the General Staff, denounced by his co-officers of the General Staff, sentenced under pressure by the Chiefs of Staff. Once again, he could not be found innocent without the entire General Staff being guilty. And so, by all means imaginable, by press campaigns, by official communications, by influence, the War Office covered up for Esterhazy only to condemn Dreyfus once again. . . . We are horrified by the terrible light the Dreyfus affair has cast upon it all, this human sacrifice of an unfortunate man, a "dirty Jew." Ah, what a cesspool of folly and foolishness, what preposterous fantasies, what corrupt police tactics, what inquisitorial, tyrannical practices! What petty whims of a few higher-ups trampling the nation under their boots, ramming back down their throats the people's cries for truth and justice, with the travesty of state security as a pretext. . . .

It is a crime that those people who wish to see a generous France take her place as leader of all the free and just nations are being accused of fomenting turmoil in the country, denounced by the very plotters who are conniving so shamelessly to foist this miscarriage of justice on the entire world. It is a crime to lie to the public, to twist public opinion to insane lengths in the service of the vilest death-dealing machinations. It is a crime to poison the minds of the meek and the humble, to stoke the passions of reactionism and intolerance, by appealing to that odious anti-Semitism that, unchecked, will destroy the freedom-loving France of the Rights of Man. It is a crime to exploit patriotism in the service of hatred, and it is, finally, a crime to ensconce the sword as the modern god, whereas all science is toiling to achieve the coming era of truth and justice.

Truth and justice, so ardently longed for! How terrible it is to see them trampled, unrecognized and ignored! . . .

This is the plain truth, Mr. President, and it is terrifying. It will leave an indelible stain on your presidency. I realize that you have no power over this case, that you are limited by the Constitution and your entourage. You have, nonetheless, your duty as a man, which you will recognize and fulfil. As for myself, I have not despaired in the least, of the triumph of right.

I repeat with the most vehement conviction: truth is on the march, and nothing will stop it. . . .

I accuse Lt. Col. du Paty de Clam of being the diabolical creator of this miscarriage of justice . . . over the last three years, by all manner of ludicrous and evil machinations.

I accuse General Mercier of complicity, at least by mental weakness, in one of the greatest inequities of the century.

I accuse General Billot of having held in his hands absolute proof of Dreyfus's innocence and covering it up, and making himself guilty of this crime against mankind and justice, as a political expedient and a way for the compromised General Staff to save face. . . .

I have but one passion: to enlighten those who have been kept in the dark, in the name of humanity which has suffered so much and is entitled to happiness. My fiery protest is simply the cry of my very soul. Let them dare, then, to bring me before a court of law and let the inquiry take place in broad daylight! I am waiting.

With my deepest respect, Sir.
Émile Zola, 13th January 1898

Lorenzo the Magnificent to his son Giovanni de Medici, 23 March 1492

Every boy of sixteen should receive a letter like this from his father, telling him to stay clear of debauchery and concentrate on his work. This one is special because the son, Giovanni, has just become the youngest-ever cardinal in the history of the Catholic Church. He already has a proven tendency to overindulge his sensual appetites in terms of both food and women. And his father is Lorenzo the Magnificent, the head of the house of Medici, a vastly wealthy banker, ruthless political player, and brilliant patron of Renaissance art who has effectively ruled the republican city-state of Florence since 1469. Now Lorenzo is older and in decline, but he has just managed to achieve his ambition to arrange the elevation of his son Giovanni to the scarlet of cardinal, which means the Medici are diversifying their power into the Church and into Rome. But that means the boy is setting off for Rome, a city rightly called a "sink of iniquity" where there are said to be seven thousand prostitutes in a population of just fifty thousand. Lorenzo is a tender father, as you can see in his wonderful letter, full of sensible advice like "Eat plain food and take plenty of exercise" and "oppose temptation." But Rome is about to become even more lascivious: the Borgias are coming to power. . . .

Just after Giovanni's departure for Rome, his magnificent father died and the Medicis temporarily lost control of Florence. Cheerful, hedonistic, and fat, Cardinal de Medici enjoyed his career in Rome, finally in 1513 contriving to be elected pope as Leo X, the very definition of the decadent, venal pontiff who inspired Martin Luther's revolt against the corrupt Church. On his election, he is said to have announced: "Since God has given us the papacy, let us enjoy it." He died in 1521 after thoroughly enjoying every minute.

> The first thing I want to impress upon you is that you ought to be grateful to God, remembering always that it is not through *your* merits, or *your* wisdom that you have gained this dignity, but through *His* favor. Show your thankfulness by a holy, exemplary, chaste life. . . . During the past year I have been much comforted to see that, without being told to do so, you have often

of your own accord gone to confession and to Holy
Communion. I do not think there is a better way of
keeping in God's grace than to make this a regular
practice. I know only too well that in going to live
in Rome, which is a sink of iniquity, you will find it
hard to follow this advice because there will be many
there who will try to corrupt you and incite you to
vice, and because your promotion to the cardinalate
at your early age arouses much envy. . . . You must,
therefore, opposite temptation all the more firmly. . . .
It is at the same time necessary that you should not
incur a reputation for hypocrisy, and in conversation
not to affect either austerity or undue seriousness. You
will understand all this better when you are older. . . .
You are well aware how important is the example you
ought to show to others as a cardinal, and that the
world would be a better place if all cardinals were what
they ought to be, because if they ever were so there
would always be a good Pope and consequently a more
peaceful world. . . .

   You are the youngest cardinal, not only in the
Sacred College of today but at any time in the past.
Therefore, when you are in assembly with other
cardinals, you must be the most unassuming, and the
most humble. . . . Try to live with regularity. . . . Silk
and jewels are seldom suitable to those in your station.
Much better to collect antiquities and beautiful books,
and to maintain a learned and well regulated household
rather than a grand one. Invite others to your house
more often than you accept invitations to theirs; but not
too often. Eat plain food and take plenty of exercise. . . .
Confide in others too little rather than too much.
One rule above all others I urge you to observe most

rigorously: *Rise early in the morning.* This is not only for your health's sake, but also so that you can arrange and expedite all the day's business. . . .

With regard to your speaking in the Consistory, I think it would be best for the present while you are still so young, to refer whatever is proposed to you to His Holiness, giving as your reason your youth and inexperience. You will find that you will be asked to intercede with the Pope for many small objects. Try at first to do this as seldom as you can, and not to worry him unduly in this way. For it is the Pope's nature to pay the most attention to those who bother him least. . . .

Farewell

Liberation

Emmeline Pankhurst to the Women's Social and Political Union, 10 January 1913

Emmeline Pankhurst demands a militant campaign to acquire votes for women, including smashing windows and arson. Pankhurst's methods appalled many, including her daughters Adela and Sylvia, who left the Women's Social and Political Union (WSPU) in protest; many other prominent activists claimed that the extremists of the WSPU "were the chief obstacles in the way of the success of the suffrage movement in the House of Commons." Nonetheless, Pankhurst's methods worked. She placed female suffrage at the center of the national agenda.

Born in Manchester, married to a much older barrister, a supporter of the female suffrage movement, with whom she had five children, Pankhurst was a highly effective campaigner. She, her daughters, and her supporters known as the Suffragettes organized violent protests and assaults on policemen, were imprisoned, went on hunger strikes, and were force-fed and beaten several times. Only the First World War stopped her protests, but ironically it was the war that made female suffrage undeniable. In 1918 votes were granted to women who were householders over the age of thirty. This was extended to women over twenty-one in 1928—just before Pankhurst's death.

LINCOLN'S INN HOUSE, KINGSWAY, W.C.
PRIVATE AND CONFIDENTIAL

Dear Friend,

The Prime Minister has announced that in the week beginning January 20th, the Women's Amendments to the Manhood Suffrage Bill will be discussed and voted upon. This means that within a few short days the fate of these Amendments will be finally decided.

The W.S.P.U. has from the first declined to call any truce on the strength of the Prime Minister's so-called pledge, and has refused to depend upon the Amendments in question, because the Government have not accepted the responsibility of getting them carried. There are, however, some Suffragists—and there may be some even in the ranks of the W.S.P.U.—who hope against hope that in spite of the Government's intrigues an unofficial Amendment may be carried. Feeling as they do, these Suffragists are tempted to hold their hand as far as militancy is concerned, until after the fate of the Amendments is known.

But every member of the W.S.P.U. recognizes that the defeat of the Amendments will make militancy more a moral duty and more a political necessity than it has ever been before. We must prepare beforehand to deal with that situation!

There are degrees of militancy. Some women are able to go further than others in militant action and each woman is the judge of her own duty so far as that is concerned. To be militant in some way or other is, however, a moral obligation. It is a duty which every woman will owe to her own conscience and self-respect, to other women who are less fortunate than she herself is, and to all those who are to come after her.

If any woman refrains from militant protest against the injury done by the Government and the House of Commons to women and to the race, she will share the responsibility for the crime. Submission under such circumstances will be itself a crime.

I know that the defeat of the Amendments will prove to thousands of women that to rely only on peaceful, patient methods, is to court failure, and that militancy is inevitable.

We must, as I have said, prepare to meet the crisis before it arises. Will you therefore tell me (by letter, if it is not possible to do so by word of mouth), that you are ready to take your share in manifesting in a practical manner your indignation at the betrayal of our cause.

Yours sincerely, E. Pankhurst

Rosa Parks to Jessica Mitford, 26 February 1956

The mother of the civil rights movement in America, Rosa Parks, then around forty-three, was already an activist along with her husband when she took on the racist law in Montgomery, Alabama, that ordered the segregation of white and black people on the local buses. This was just one of the notorious "Jim Crow" laws brought in throughout the Southern states in the early twentieth century, enforcing repression of black people even though slavery had been abolished forty years earlier. Parks had helped investigate some of the racist atrocities—gang rapes and murders of people of color—that so often went unpunished in Alabama.

In December 1955 Parks refused to give up her seat in the

"colored" section of the bus she was traveling in to a white pas-
senger when the "white" section was full. She was arrested, and
her case was used in the subsequent legal challenge against segregation that was won in November 1956. In the middle of the
case, before its outcome is known, Parks writes this letter to
"Mrs. Treuhaft," who is better known as Jessica Mitford, the
most radical of the six daughters of the English nobleman Lord
Redesdale. One became a duchess, two were Nazi sympathiz-
ers, one was a novelist, and Jessica became a Communist. At
this time she is married to Robert Treuhaft, a civil rights lawyer living in California. This story is not over. This letter marks
just one stage in the long history of the struggle against racism
in America, starting with the American Civil War, continuing
with the work of Martin Luther King Jr. in the 1960s—and
essential today with movements like Black Lives Matter.

Dear Mrs. Treuhaft:
    I am very happy to hear from you again. Thanks,
very much for the contribution and the names of other
contributors.
    We are having a difficult time here, but we are not
discouraged. The increased pressure seems to strengthen
us for the next blow.
    My first case was heard in the Circuit Court
February 22, I was found guilty and sentenced to
70 days in jail. The appeal was made to the State
Supreme Court.
    I was immediately arrested again with the leaders of
the bus protest.
    We have received very generous contributions from
over the country, although no specific appeal has been
made through the mail.

The wide spread publicity we are getting is most
disturbing to the local governing group. They resent
outside interference. Therefore, I will have to take
the matter of direct appeal to the Montgomery
Improvement Association.

The Claudette Colvin Case is one of four filed with
the Federal Court at present.

I will write again soon.

Sincerely yours,
Rosa L. Parks

Nelson Mandela to Winnie Mandela, 2 April 1969

Mandela's prison letters to Winnie are lessons on how to live.
Born into Tembu royalty in 1918, Mandela joined the African
National Congress and the armed struggle against apartheid as
a lawyer in Johannesburg in the 1950s. Seven years later Nelson
spotted a young woman, Winnie Madikizela, aged twenty-two,
at a bus stop. Divorcing his wife, he married Winnie. At the
Rivonia Trial in 1964 Mandela was sentenced to life imprison-
ment for terrorism.

Mandela's inspirational prison letters show his gift for self-
improvement, his astonishing humility and natural decency.
During twenty-seven years in prison, as he explains to Winnie
here, Mandela regards his cell as "an ideal place to learn to
know yourself, to search realistically and regularly the process
of your own mind and feelings. In judging our progress as indi-
viduals we tend to concentrate on external factors such as one's
social position, influence and popularity, wealth and standard
of education. These are, of course, important . . . and it is per-

fectly understandable if many people exert themselves mainly to achieve all these. But internal factors may be even more crucial in assessing one's development as a human being. Honesty, sincerity, simplicity, humility, pure generosity, absence of vanity, readiness to serve others—qualities which are within easy reach of every soul—are the foundation of one's spiritual life. Development in matters of this nature is inconceivable without serious introspection, without knowing yourself, your weaknesses and mistakes. At least, if for nothing else, the cell gives you the opportunity to look daily into your entire conduct, to overcome the bad and develop whatever is good in you. Regular meditation, say about 15 minutes a day before you turn in, can be very fruitful in this regard. You may find it difficult at first to pinpoint the negative features in your life, but the 10th attempt may yield rich rewards. Never forget that a saint is a sinner who keeps on trying."

During his long ordeal, Winnie struggled without his guidance, enforcing her power in Soweto through a security unit of murderous thugs called the Mandela United Football Team. Released in 1990 and then elected president, Mandela oversaw the transfer of power from white rule to multiracial democracy without bloodshed—one of the towering achievements of the twentieth century.

Mandela divorced Winnie in 1992 and married Graça, the widow of President Machel of Mozambique. Mandela died in 2013, Winnie five years later. This letter, signed "Dalibunga," his Xhosa tribal name, is one of his best.

Darling,
    I was taken completely by surprise to learn that you had been very unwell as I did not have even the slightest hint that you suffered from blackouts. I

have known of your heart condition & pleurisy attacks.

The Power of Positive Thinking & The Results of Positive Thinking, both written by the American psychologist Dr. Norman Vincent Peale, may be rewarding to read.

He makes the basic point that it is not so much the disability one suffers from that matters but one's attitude to it. The man who says: I will conquer this illness & live a happy life, is already halfway to victory.

Of the talents you possess, the one that attracts me most is your courage & determination. This makes you stand head & shoulders above the average & will in the end bring you the triumph of high achievement. Do consciously keep this constantly in mind.

You look somewhat sad, absent-minded & unwell but lovely all the same [in a family photo]. The [photo] depicts all I know in you, the devastating beauty & charm which ten stormy years of married life have not chilled. I suspect that you intended the picture to convey a special message that no words could ever express. Rest assured I have caught it. All that I wish to say now is that the picture has aroused all the tender feelings in me & softened the grimness that is all around. It has sharpened my longing for you & our sweet & peaceful home.

Finally Mhlope, I should like you to know that if in the past my letters have not been passionate, it is because I need not seek to improve the debt I owe to a woman who, in spite of formidable difficulties & lack of experience, has nonetheless succeeded in keeping the home fires burning & in attending to the smallest wants & wishes of her incarcerated life companion. These things make me humble to be the object of your love & affection. Remember that hope is a powerful weapon even when all else is lost. You are in my thoughts every moment of my life. Nothing will happen to you darling. You will certainly recover and rise.

A million kisses & tons & tons of love.
Dalibunga

Abram Hannibal to Peter the Great, 5 March 1722

The first black general and engineer of modern times was a Russian African named Abram Hannibal. He was captured by slave traders as a boy, probably in West Africa; sold in Istanbul, and there bought by agents of Tsar Peter the Great, who brought him to Russia where "I was baptized by the Tsar-Emperor and His Majesty chose to stand as my godfather." Henceforth he was known as Abram Petrovich ("Son of Peter") Hannibal because many black men were called "Hannibal" after the Carthaginian general (though in fact he was Phoenician). Hannibal often served as Peter's equerry; the tsar recognized the boy's talent, sending him to be trained in engineering, artillery, and mathematics in Paris, where he ran out of money. Here Hannibal appeals to Peter, who bails him out, ordering his chancellor: "Abram the Moor has written from Paris that he is ready to come back to Russia only he has to settle debts of 200 gold écu. . . . Please send money and travel expenses and tell Abram to leave for Petersburg." By Catherine the Great's reign, Hannibal was a general; he was the great-grandfather of the poet Pushkin.

Do you remember Your Majesty how you warned me
five years ago not to fall into bad habits or end up in
prison. Instead you told me if I worked hard at my
studies for the glory of Russia you would never desert
me. Well I didn't let you down but we are all of us in
debt here not because of delinquency on our party but
simply we are victims of paper money with terrible
consequences as I am sure Count Musin Pushkin told
you were it not for his kindness I would have surely
died of hunger.

Between Simón Bolívar, Manuela Sáenz, and James Thorne, 1822–1823

Here are two goodbye letters in the love triangle of the Liberator of South America. "I am the genius of the storm," declared
Simón Bolívar, known as El Libertador, who in a just a few
frantic years of fighting the Spanish, freed the modern states
of Colombia, Venezuela, Panama, Ecuador, Peru, and Bolivia—
half of a vast continent. Only Napoleon Bonaparte had achieved
anything resembling the conquests of Bolívar. But he was also
an enthusiastic dancer and lover, often greeted by devoted
young girls as he liberated their cities, claiming that sex and
flirtation stimulated his genius: "I deliberated best when I was
at the center of revelry among the pleasures of a ball." And the
genius of the storm met his match in Manuela Sáenz.

After becoming president of Gran Colombia in 1819,
Bolívar marched across the Andes to conquer Ecuador where
he met twenty-two-year-old Manuela, the illegitimate daughter of a Spanish nobleman and a mixed-race mother, a convent
girl who had been seduced by an officer, then married off to
James Thorne, an older English merchant. Flamboyant, fear-

less, intelligent, and sensuous, she became Bolívar's supporter and lover. But Bolívar fears any commitment, sounding much like anyone feeling suffocated in a relationship: "give me time." He tries to restrain Manuela's enthusiasm and sends her back to her husband.

Simón Bolívar to Manuela Sáenz, 3 July 1822

I want to answer, most beautiful Manuela, your
demands of love, which are entirely reasonable. But
I have to be candid with you, who have given me so
much of yourself . . . it's time you knew that long
ago I loved a woman as only the young can love. Out
of respect, I never talk about it. I'm pondering these
things, and I want to give you time to do the same,
because your words lure me; because I know that this
may well be my moment to love you and for us to
love one another. I need time to get used to this, for
a military life is neither easy to endure nor easy to
leave behind. I have fooled death so many times now
that death dogs my every step. . . . Allow me to be
sure of myself—of you. . . . I cannot lie. I never lie!
My passion for you is wild, and you know it. Give me
time.

And here is Manuela's response: she writes this amazing letter to her husband, copying it to Bolívar to make sure there is no way back to her tedious marriage: her destiny is with Bolívar, whom she then follows to Bogotá.

Manuela Sáenz to James Thorne, 1823

No, no, no, hombre! A thousand times No! Sir, you
are an excellent person, indeed one of a kind—that I
will never deny. I only regret that you are not a better
man so that my leaving you would honor Bolívar more.
I know very well that I can never be joined to him
in what you call honor. Do you think I am any less
honorable because he is my lover, not my husband?
Ah! I do not live by social conventions men construct
to torment us. So leave me be, my dear Englishman.
We will marry again in heaven but not on this
earth. . . . On earth, you are a boring man. Up there
in the celestial heights, everything will be so English,
because a life of monotony was invented for you
people, who make love without pleasure, conversation
without grace—who walk slowly, greet solemnly, move
heavily, joke without laughing. . . . But enough of my
cheekiness. With all the sobriety, truth, and clarity of
an Englishwoman, I say now: I will never return for
you. You are a protestant and I a pagan—that should
be obstacle enough. But I am also in love with another
man, and that is the greater, stronger reason. You see
how precise my mind can be?

Your invariable friend, Manuela

Manuela fought beside Bolívar, helped with his papers,
nursed the wounded, and deserved her promotion to colonel.
There was something utterly liberated about Manuela: she
sported dashing male uniforms, had affairs with black servants
and female lovers, defied all convention. In Bogotá's presi-

dential palace in 1828, assassins forced their way into Bolívar's bedroom. Manuela fought them off and was almost beaten to death, enabling The Liberator to escape. Henceforth he called her "Libertadora de Libertador"—the liberatrix of the liberator. Bolívar retired from power and died of tuberculosis, aged forty-seven, in 1830. Manuela, persecuted, died in penury in 1856. In 2007, she was posthumously promoted to a general of Ecuador and in 2010 given a state funeral in Venezuela.

Fate

Oscar Wilde to Robert Ross, 28 February 1895

Even though he didn't yet know it, this letter marks the beginning of the ruin of Oscar Wilde. The author of *The Importance of Being Earnest, The Picture of Dorian Gray,* and stories for children and adults such as "The Happy Prince," Wilde was celebrated for his wit and his success. When he arrived in America, he told the customs officials "I have nothing to declare but my genius," then made a fortune on a sold-out lecture tour. Son of a Dublin surgeon, Wilde was married with children but he was also ostentatiously gay at a time when homosexuality was illegal. He loved the adventure of pursuing wild encounters, which he called "feasting with panthers," but he was in love with a spoiled aristocrat named Lord Alfred "Bosie" Douglas, whose monstrous father, the Marquess of Queensberry, was a pugilistic and bigoted ruffian. On this day, Queensberry left a provocative and misspelled card at Wilde's club, calling him a "Somdomite." In this letter, Wilde reports Queensberry's insult to his best friend, literary executor, and sometime lover Robbie Ross, who like everyone else begs him not to take the bait. But Wilde insists on suing Queensberry for libel, a folly that would lead inexorably to his exposure as a homosexual, his trial, and his sentencing to prison with hard labor: it destroyed him.

HOTEL AVONDALE, PICCADILLY

Dearest Bobbie,

Since I saw you something has happened. Bosie's
father has left a card at my club with hideous words on
it. I don't see anything but a criminal prosecution.

My whole life seems ruined by this man. The tower
of ivory is assailed by the foul thing. On the sand is my
life spilled. I don't know what to do. If you could come
here at 11:30 please do so tonight. I mar your life by
trespassing ever on your love and kindness. I have asked
Bosie to come tomorrow.

Ever yours
Oscar

Between Alexander Hamilton and Aaron Burr, June 1804

The letters that follow chart the destruction of the most brilliant
mind of the American Founding Fathers by the most despicable. The musical *Hamilton* has retold the story using hip-hop
music, but here are the real letters. Alexander Hamilton was
the illegitimate prodigy born on a Caribbean island who made
it to America, became aide to George Washington, designer
of the American Constitution, and the first treasury secretary
as well as an army general. He possessed all the turbulence
of genius but also, in an era obsessed with a complex code of
honor, the touchiness of the self-invented.

Aaron Burr, also a veteran of the War of Independence, had
all Hamilton's ambition but lacked his brilliance, and he seethed

with jealousy, particularly when Hamilton helped undermine his career by backing his old enemy Thomas Jefferson against him, Burr, his supposed friend, in the presidential elections of 1800. Burr was instead elected vice president under Jefferson, but the president despised and excluded him. Hamilton himself was out of power after the collapse of his Federalist Party. Using the orotund language of honor and law (both being lawyers), Burr accuses Hamilton of defaming him in the 1804 contest for the governorship of New York. Under the exaggeratedly polite phrases the reader can feel the oncoming resort to violence—in the form of a duel—and then we read the arrangements being made by their seconds, William P. Van Ness and Nathaniel Pendleton.

The duel is fought on 11 July 1804, in New Jersey. Hamilton claimed he would fire in the air. Burr shoots at Hamilton, killing him. Burr was charged with his murder, but was never tried. He lived on until 1836, perhaps the most despised man in early American history.

Burr to Hamilton

N YORK 18 JUNE 1804

Sir,

I send for your perusal a letter signed Ch. D. Cooper which, though apparently published some time ago, has but very recently come to my knowledge. Mr. Van Ness, who does me the favor to deliver this, will point out to you that clause of the letter to which I particularly request your attention.

You must perceive, Sir, the necessity of a prompt and unqualified acknowledgment or denial of the use of

any expressions which could warrant the assertions of
Dr. Cooper.

> *I have the honor to be*
> Your Obdt. St.
> A. Burr

Hamilton to Burr

N YORK 20 JUNE 1804

Sir:

I have maturely reflected on the subject of your
letter of the 18th Instant, and the more I have reflected,
the more I have become convinced that I could not
without manifest impropriety make the avowal or
disavowal which you seem to think necessary. The
clause pointed out by Mr. Van Ness is in these terms:
"I could detail to you a still more despicable opinion
which General Hamilton has expressed of Mr. Burr." To
endeavor to discover the meaning of this declaration, I
was obliged to seek in the antecedent part of the letter
for the opinion to which it referred, as having been
already disclosed. I found it in these words: "Genl.
Hamilton and Judge Kent have declared in substance
that they looked upon Mr. Burr to be a dangerous man,
and one who ought not to be trusted with the reins
of Government." The language of Dr. Cooper plainly
implies that he considered this opinion of you, which
he attributes to me, as a despicable one; but he affirms
that I have expressed some other still more despicable;
without, however, mentioning to whom, when or where.
'Tis evident that the phrase "still more despicable"

admits of infinite shades from very light to very dark. How am I to judge of the degree intended. Or how should I annex any precise idea to language so vague?

Between Gentlemen despicable and still more despicable are not worth the pains of a distinction. When, therefore, you do not interrogate me as to the opinion which is specifically ascribed to me, I must conclude that you view it as within the limits to which the animadversions of political opponents, upon each other, may justifiably extend; and consequently as not warranting the idea of it which Dr. Cooper appears to entertain. If so, what precise inference could you draw as a guide for your future conduct, were I to acknowledge that I had expressed an opinion of you, still more despicable than the one which is particularized? How could you be sure that even this opinion had exceeded the bounds which you would yourself deem admissible between political opponents?

But I forbear further comment on the embarrassment to which the requisition you have made naturally leads. The occasion forbids a more ample illustration, though nothing would be more easy than to pursue it.

Repeating that I can not reconcile it with propriety to make the acknowledgment or denial you desire, I will add that I deem it inadmissible on principle, to consent to be interrogated as to the justness of the inferences which may be drawn by others, from whatever I may have said of a political opponent in the course of a fifteen years competition. If there were no other objection to it, this is sufficient, that it would tend to expose my sincerity and delicacy to

injurious imputations from every person who may at
any time have conceived that import of my expressions
differently from what I may then have intended, or may
afterward recollect.

I stand ready to avow or disavow promptly and
explicitly any precise or definite opinion which I may
be charged with having declared to any gentleman.
More than this can not fitly be expected from me; and
especially it can not reasonably be expected that I shall
enter into an explanation upon a basis so vague as that
which you have adopted. I trust upon more reflection
you will see the matter in the same light with me. If
not, I can only regret the circumstances and must abide
the consequences.

The publication of Dr. Cooper was never seen by me
'till after the receipt of your letter.

Sir, I have the honor to be
Your Obdt. St.
A. Hamilton

Burr to Hamilton

N YORK 21 JUNE 1804

Sir,

Your letter of the 20th inst. has been this day
received. Having considered it attentively, I regret to
find in it nothing of that sincerity and delicacy which
you profess to value.

Political opposition can never absolve gentlemen
from the necessity of a rigid adherence to the laws of

honor and the rules of decorum. I neither claim such privilege nor indulge it in others.

The common sense of mankind affixes to the epithet adopted by Dr. Cooper the idea of dishonor. It has been publicly applied to me under the sanction of your name. The question is not whether he has understood the meaning of the word or has used it according to syntax and with grammatical accuracy, but whether you have authorized this application either directly or by uttering expression or opinion derogatory to my honor. The time "when" is in your own knowledge but no way material to me, as the calumny has now just been disclosed so as to become the subject of my notice and as the effect is present and palpable.

Your letter has furnished me with new reasons for requiring a definite reply.

> *I have the honor to be*
> Your Obdt. St.
> A. Burr

Hamilton to Burr

N YORK 22 JUNE 1804

Sir,

Your first letter, in a style too peremptory, made a demand, in my opinion, unprecedented and unwarrantable. My answer, pointing out the embarrassment, gave you an opportunity to take a less exceptionable course. You have not chosen to do it, but by your last letter, received this day, containing expressions indecorous and improper, you have increased the difficulties to explanation, intrinsically incident to the nature of your application.

If by a "definite reply" you mean the direct avowal or disavowal required in your first letter, I have no other answer to give than that which has already been given. If you mean anything different admitting of greater latitude, it is requisite you should explain.

> *I have the honor to be, Sir*
> Your Obdt. St.
> A. Hamilton

Van Ness to Pendleton, 26 June 1804

Sir,

The letter which you yesterday delivered me and your subsequent communication in Col. Burr's opinion evince no disposition on the part of Genl. Hamilton to come to a satisfactory accommodation. The injury complained of and the reparation expected are so definitely expressed in his (Col. B.'s) letter of the 21st Inst. that there is not perceived a necessity for further explanation on his part. The difficulty that would result from confining the inquiry to any particular times and occasions must be manifest. The denial of a specified conversation only, would leave strong implications that on other occasions improper language had been used. When and where injurious expressions and opinions have been uttered by Genl. Hamilton must be best known to him and of him only does Col. Burr think it proper to inquire.

No denial or declaration will be satisfactory unless it be general so as to wholly exclude the idea that rumors derogatory to Col. Burr's honor can have originated with Genl. Hamilton or have been fairly inferred from anything he has said. A definite reply to a requisition of this nature is demanded in Col. Burr's letter of the 21st Inst. This being refused, invites the alternative alluded to in Genl. H.'s letter of the 20th Inst. It was demanded by the position in which the controversy was placed by Genl. H. on the 22nd Inst., and I was immediately furnished with a communication demanding a personal interview.

The necessity of this measure has not in the opinion of Col. Burr been diminished by the General's last letter or any subsequent communication which has been received and I am again instructed to deliver you a message as soon as it may be convenient for you to receive it. I beg, therefore, you will have the politeness to inform me at what hour I shall wait on you.

> *Your most obt. & very hum. Servt.*
> W. P. Van Ness

Anonymous to Lord Monteagle, October 1605

The plan was to change the course of English history in the most nihilistic and diabolical way imaginable. After struggling for years during the long Protestant reign of Elizabeth I, a terror-ist cell of Anglo-Catholics led by Robert Catesby lost patience with the new king James I and conspired to plant gunpowder beneath the Houses of Parliament so as to murder the entire elite of the kingdom: king, queen, princes, lords, and gentlemen, a crime that would have been considerably more horrific and effective than 9/11. The cell was small enough to succeed and might easily have done so had not one of its members delivered a warning letter, anonymously, to Lord Monteagle. Having recently nearly lost his head as a participant in Lord Essex's rebellion against Queen Elizabeth, Monteagle rushes the letter to the chief minister Robert Cecil, earl of Salisbury, who shows it to the king. Cecil allows the pompous monarch the credit for interpreting the key words "terrible blow" and for ordering a search that reveals the cellar filled with gunpowder, guarded by the conspirator and explosives expert Guy Fawkes. The plot is foiled, the terrorists executed, and their failure still celebrated every year with bonfires on 5 November: Guy Fawkes Day.

My Lord, out of the love I bear to some of your friends,
I have a care of your preservation. Therefore I would
advise you, as you tender your life, to devise some
excuse to shift your attendance at this Parliament;
for God and man hath concurred to punish the
wickedness of this time. And think not slightly of this
advertisement, but retire yourself into your country
where you may expect the event in safety. For though
there be no appearance of any stir, yet I say they shall
receive a terrible blow this Parliament; and yet they
shall not see who hurts them. This counsel is not to be
condemned because it may do you good and can do
you no harm; for the danger is passed as soon as you
have burnt the letter. And I hope God will give you the
grace to make good use of it, to whose holy protection I
commend you.

Babur to Humayun, 25 December 1526

The targets of assassination attempts often die. Sometimes they survive, but they rarely write a detailed letter about the experience and their vengeance. But then, there are very few characters as extraordinary as Babur, the first emperor of Mughal India, conqueror, poet, memoirist, lover. In 1526 he invades India. He captures Delhi and kills the ruling sultan of the Lodi dynasty, Ibrahim, in battle. But he spares Ibrahim's mother, Buwa, and allows her to live on in the palace. Typically Babur decides to try Indian food and keeps four Indian chefs to do so. When Buwa hears this, she persuades the imperial chefs to poison the new emperor. Somehow Babur survives. His enemies had plotted his downfall. Instead it heralds their own: as he explains, he devises terrible deaths for the four assassins. The whole episode is recounted in a unique letter to his son Humayun, who then rules his Afghan territories from Kabul in Babur's own flamboyant and vivid style.

> On Friday the sixteenth of Rabi [21 December] a
> strange incident took place. . . . The wretched Buwa,
> mother of Ibrahim, heard that I was eating foods
> prepared by Hindustani cooks. This came about because
> three or four months prior to this date, since I had
> never seen Hindustani food, I said that Ibrahim's cooks
> should be brought. Of fifty or sixty cooks I kept four.
> So, having heard of this, she sent a man to Etawah
> to obtain a tola of poison wrapped up in a piece of
> paper and then give it to an old woman servant,
> who would then pass it to Ahmad Chashnigir. (In
> Hindustan they call the taster *chashnigir*, and a tola
> is a measure slightly more than two mithcals, as has

been described.) Ahmad gave it to the Hindustani
cook in our kitchen, promising him four parganas to
introduce it somehow to my food. After the first old
woman, who gave Ahmad Chashnigir the poison, she
sent another to see whether or not he had given me
the poison. It is good that he put it on the plate and
not in the pot, having done so because I had given the
cooks strict instructions to supervise the Hindustanis
and make them taste from the pot while our food was
being prepared. When the meal was being dished out,
however, our wretched cooks were negligent. The cook
put a piece of thin bread on the porcelain plate and
then sprinkled less than half of the poison from the
paper on top of the bread. On top of the poison he put
some meat dressed in oil. If he had sprinkled the poison
on the meat, or if he had thrown it into the pot, it
would have been bad. In a fluster, he threw the rest into
the stove.

Late Friday evening they served the food. I ate a lot
of rabbit stew and had quite a bit of dressed saffroned
meat. I also had one or two tidbits from the top of the
poisoned Hindustani food. I took the dressed meat
and ate it. There was no apparent bad taste. I had one
or two pieces of dried meat. I felt sick. The day before,
when I was eating dried meat, there had been an off-
taste, so I thought that was the reason. Once again my
stomach churned. While seated at the meal I felt sick
two or three times and almost threw up. Finally I said
to myself, "Enough of this." I got up and on my way to
the toilet I almost threw up once. When I got to the
toilet I vomited a lot. I never vomited after meals, not
even when drinking. A cloud of suspicion came over
my mind. I ordered the cook to be held while the vomit

was given to a dog that was watched. Until near the end
of the first watch the next morning the dog was pretty
listless and its stomach was swollen. No matter how
many stones they threw at it to try and get it to move,
it refused to get up. It remained like that until midday,
but then it got up and did not die. One or two pages
had eaten the same food, and the next morning they
too threw up a lot. One was very ill, but in the end they
all recovered completely. "Calamity struck, but all's well
that ends well." God gave me life anew; I had returned
from the brink of death; I was born again. "Wounded,
I died and came to life again, Now I have learned the
value of life." I ordered Sultan-Muhammad Bakhshï to
keep a close watch on the cook. When he was tortured
he confessed the details given above.

On Monday I ordered the nobles, grandees, amirs,
and ministers to attend court. The two men and two
women were brought in for questioning. They confessed
to all the details of the affair. I ordered the taster to be
hacked to pieces and the cook to be skinned alive. One
of the two women I had thrown under the elephants'
feet, and the other I had shot. I had Buwa put under
arrest. She will pay for what she has done.

On Saturday I drank a cup of milk. On Sunday I
drank a cup of milk. I also drank some earth of Lemnos
and opiate in milk and drank it. The milk really shook
up my insides. On Saturday, the first day of this
medication, I excreted some pitch-black things like
burnt bile. Thank goodness now everything is all right.
I never knew how precious life was. There is a line of
poetry that says, "He who reaches the point of death
appreciates life." Every time I think of this dreadful
incident I get angry. It was by God's grace that I

was given a new lease on life. How can I express my
thanks?

Hoping this will not occasion alarm, I have
described in detail everything that happened. Although
it was a dreadful incident that cannot be adequately
described by words, thank God I have lived to see
another day, and all's well that ends well. Do not
worry.

Nikita Khrushchev to John F. Kennedy, 24 & 26 October 1962

Two letters: one almost brings the world to the brink of nuclear
annihilation, and the other brings it back. When US spy planes
spot Soviet nuclear missiles on the Communist-ruled island of
Cuba, President John F. Kennedy faces probably the greatest
crisis confronted by any commander-in-chief. America cannot
allow the missiles to remain there and threaten American cities, yet any attempt to remove them may spark apocalyptic war.
The young president imposes a blockade on the island, turning
back further Soviet ships. The Soviet leader, Nikita Khrushchev, writes an aggressive letter that threatens war. The crisis
darkens.

Two days later, a second, more conciliatory letter from Khrushchev arrives. Kennedy agonizes over their meanings. Finally,
Kennedy decides to ignore the aggressive letter and simply
answer the conciliatory one. A deal is agreed: Khrushchev is to
withdraw his missiles and Kennedy is to never invade Cuba—
and to secretly remove US missiles from Turkey. If for nothing
else, Kennedy's conduct justifies his reputation. As for Cuba,
its Marxist leader Fidel Castro had been willing to risk nuclear
catastrophe and never forgave Khrushchev's betrayal. As for

Khrushchev, his comrades were infuriated by his erratic reck-
lessness and overthrew him a few months later.

MOSCOW, OCTOBER 24, 1962

Dear Mr. President: I have received your letter of
October 23, I have studied it, and am answering you.

Just imagine, Mr. President, that we had presented
you with the conditions of an ultimatum which you
have presented us by your action. How would you
have reacted to this? I think that you would have been
indignant at such a step on our part. And this would
have been understandable to us.

In presenting us with these conditions, you, Mr.
President, have flung a challenge at us. Who asked you
to do this? By what right did you do this? . . .

You, Mr. President, are not declaring a quarantine,
but rather are setting forth an ultimatum and
threatening that if we do not give in to your demands
you will use force. Consider what you are saying! And
you want to persuade me to agree to this! . . .

No, Mr. President, I cannot agree to this, and I
think that in your own heart you recognize that I am
correct. I am convinced that in my place you would act
the same way. . . .

And we also say—no. . . .

The Soviet Government considers that the
violation of the freedom to use international waters
and international air space is an act of aggression
which pushes mankind toward the abyss of a world
nuclear-missile war. Therefore, the Soviet Government
cannot instruct the captains of Soviet vessels bound for
Cuba to observe the orders of American naval forces

blockading that Island. Our instructions to Soviet mariners are to observe strictly the universally accepted norms of navigation in international waters and not to retreat one step from them. And if the American side violates these rules, it must realize what responsibility will rest upon it in that case. Naturally we will not simply be bystanders with regard to piratical acts by American ships on the high seas. We will then be forced on our part to take the measures we consider necessary and adequate in order to protect our rights. We have everything necessary to do so.

Respectfully,
N. Khrushchev

MOSCOW, OCTOBER 26, 1962, 7 P.M.

Dear Mr. President:

I have received your letter of October 25. From your letter, I got the feeling that you have some understanding of the situation which has developed and (some) sense of responsibility. I value this. . . .

I think you will understand me correctly if you are really concerned about the welfare of the world. Everyone needs peace. . . . War is our enemy and a calamity for all the peoples. . . .

I see, Mr. President, that you too are not devoid of a sense of anxiety for the fate of the world understanding, and of what war entails. What would a war give you? You are threatening us with war. . . .

In the name of the Soviet Government and the Soviet people, I assure you that your conclusions regarding offensive weapons on Cuba are groundless. . . .

You are mistaken if you think that any of our means on Cuba are offensive. However, let us not quarrel now. It is apparent that I will not be able to convince you of this. . . .

But, Mr. President, do you really seriously think that Cuba can attack the United States and that even we together with Cuba can attack you from the territory of Cuba? Can you really think that way? How is it possible? We do not understand this. . . .

If you are really concerned about the peace and welfare of your people, and this is your responsibility as President, then I, as the Chairman of the Council of Ministers, am concerned for my people. Moreover, the preservation of world peace should be our joint concern, since if, under contemporary conditions, war should break out, it would be a war not only between the reciprocal claims, but a worldwide cruel and destructive war. . . .

If assurances were given by the President and the Government of the United States that the USA itself would not participate in an attack on Cuba and would restrain others from actions of this sort, if you would recall your fleet, this would immediately change everything. . . . Then too, the question of the destruction, not only of the armaments which you call offensive, but of all other armaments as well, would look different. . . .

Let us therefore show statesmanlike wisdom. I propose: We, for our part, will declare that our ships, bound for Cuba, will not carry any kind of armaments. You would declare that the United States will not invade Cuba with its forces and will not support any sort of forces which might intend to carry out an

invasion of Cuba. Then the necessity for the presence of
our military specialists in Cuba would disappear. . . .

If you did this as the first step towards the unleashing
of war, well then, it is evident that nothing else is left to
us but to accept this challenge of yours. If, however, you
have not lost your self-control and sensibly conceive
what this might lead to, then, Mr. President, we and
you ought not now to pull on the ends of the rope
in which you have tied the knot of war, because the
more the two of us pull, the tighter that knot will be
tied. And a moment may come when that knot will
be tied so tight that even he who tied it will not have
the strength to untie it, and then it will be necessary
to cut that knot, and what that would mean is not for
me to explain to you, because you yourself understand
perfectly of what terrible forces our countries dispose.

Consequently, if there is no intention to tighten that
knot and thereby to doom the world to the catastrophe
of thermonuclear war, then let us not only relax the
forces pulling on the ends of the rope, let us take
measures to untie that knot. . . .

There, Mr. President, are my thoughts, which, if
you agreed with them, could put an end to that tense
situation which is disturbing all peoples.

These thoughts are dictated by a sincere desire to
relieve the situation, to remove the threat of war.

Respectfully yours,
N. Khrushchev

Alexander Pushkin to Jacob von Heeckeren,
25 January 1837

The letter that led to the tragic death of Russia's sublime poet Pushkin. The great-grandson of Abram Hannibal, Peter the Great's black aide, Pushkin found himself in trouble with the tsars as soon as he started writing his outrageous, passionate, and beautiful verses. Alexander I punished him by exiling him from Petersburg to south Russia, but even there Pushkin associated with liberals, seduced the wife of the tsar's viceroy, and pursued many other love affairs until he was finally allowed home by the new tsar, the grandiloquent Nicholas I, who offered to be his personal censor.

By this time Pushkin was writing his masterpiece, the verse-novel *Eugene Onegin,* and had married Natalia, a society beauty who immediately attracted the flirtatious attentions of the tsar himself (which Pushkin had to tolerate) and of a shallow French popinjay serving in the Russian Guards named Baron Charles d'Anthes. He was the adopted son and (probable) homosexual lover of the Dutch ambassador Baron Heeckeren, who paid all his expenses. Already tormented with jealousy, Pushkin, now aged thirty-seven, receives a malicious anonymous letter from "THE SUPREME COMMANDER AND KNIGHTS OF THE MOST SERENE ORDER OF CUCKOLDS." The proud Pushkin immediately—and probably wrongly—suspects d'Anthes of cuckolding him. The tsar tries to prevent a duel, but Pushkin, determined on satisfaction, proceeds to make confrontation inevitable with this blisteringly rude letter to Heeckeren accusing him of acting as "the pimp of your son . . . like an obscene old woman." His son had to defend his adopted father's honor. In the subsequent duel, d'Anthes shot and killed Russia's most beloved poet. D'Anthes had to leave Russia—but later rose to the rank of a senator in France.

Baron!

Allow me to sum up what has just taken place. Your son's behavior had long been known to me and could not be a matter of indifference to me. I contented myself with the role of an observer, entitled to intervene when I judged it proper. An incident which at any other moment would have been very disagreeable, happily supervened to get me out of the difficulty: I received anonymous letters. You know the rest: I made your son play such a pitiable role that my wife, astonished at such cowardice and servility, could not refrain from laughing, and any emotion which she had perhaps come to feel for this great and sublime passion evaporated into the calmest and most merited disgust.

I am obliged to admit, Baron, that your role has not been altogether seemly. You, the representative of a crowned head, have been paternally the pimp of your son. It appears that all his behavior (clumsy enough, moreover) has been directed by you. It was probably you who dictated to him the sorry witticisms he has been mouthing and the twaddle he has taken upon himself to write. Like an obscene old woman, you would go and spy on my wife from every corner to speak to her of the love of your bastard, or the one so-called; and when, ill with the pox, he was confined to his home, you would say that he was dying of love for her; you would mumble: give me back my son.

You will be well aware, Baron, that after all this I cannot permit my family to have the least relation with yours. It was on this condition that I consented

not to pursue this filthy affair and not to dishonor
you in the eyes of our court and of yours, as I had the
power and intention to do. I do not care for my wife to
hear again your paternal exhortations. I cannot allow
your son, after the despicable conduct he has shown,
to dare to speak to my wife, still less to mouth to her
these barrack-room calembours, and play devotion and
unhappy passion whilst he is nothing but a coward and
a scoundrel. I am thus obliged to address myself to you,
to beg you to put an end to all these goings-on, if you
wish to avoid a new scandal, from which I certainly
shall not shrink.

I have the honor to be, Baron
Your most humble and obedient servant,
Alexander Pushkin

Power

Stalin to Valery Mezhlauk, April 1930

Gallows humor is Stalin's favorite kind. Here at a meeting of the Politburo, he sends a note around the table suggesting an appropriate punishment for the sins of the People's Commissar for Finance, Nikolai Bryukhanov, whom Stalin regarded as politically unreliable. His comrade Valery Mezhlauk, in charge of economic planning and a fine cartoonist, sketches this picture of the punishment—presumably to general amusement. The commissar was sacked and both Bryukhanov and Mezhlauk were later executed by Stalin.

For all new, existing and
future sins, to be hung by
the balls, and if the balls are
strong and don't break, to
forgive him and think correct
but if they break, then
to throw him into a river.

Наркомфин СССР
на второй день
испытания.

Winston Churchill to Franklin D. Roosevelt, 20 May 1940

An appeal for help at the supreme crisis of the Second World War. Churchill has been prime minister for just ten days. France is defeated. Britain stands alone against Nazi Europe, awaiting Hitler's invasion—and America is still neutral. Churchill asks the American president, Franklin D. Roosevelt, to sell him fifty warships to aid in defending the country, but then hears that the US ambassador to London, Joseph Kennedy, a notorious appeaser, has advised against this because Britain is about to collapse. This provokes one of Churchill's most defiant letters of British resolve:

> Our intention is, whatever happens, to fight on to the end in this Island and provided we can get the help for which we ask, we hope to run them very close in the air battles in view of individual superiority. Members of the present administration would likely go down during the process should it result adversely, but in no conceivable circumstances will we consent to surrender. If members of the present administration were finished and others came to parlay amid the ruins, you must not be blind to the fact that the sole remaining bargaining counter would be the fleet, and if this country was left by the United States to its fate, no one would have the right to blame those responsible if they made the best terms they could for the surviving inhabitants. Excuse me, Mr. President, putting this nightmare bluntly. I could not answer for my successors who in utter despair and hopelessness might well have to accommodate themselves to the German will. However there is no

need at present to dwell upon such ideas. Once more thanking you for your good will.

Between Richard I and Saladin, October–November 1191

Here is an attempt to negotiate a peace process by partition of the Holy Land in the late twelfth century. At this time Saladin, the Kurdish-born Islamic sultan of Syria and Egypt, has defeated the Crusader kingdom of Jerusalem and retaken the Holy City. But he has failed to retake the city of Acre where a new crusade has landed, led by the formidable Christian warrior King Richard I of England—the Lionheart. Fighting themselves to a stalemate, the two now propose to share the present state of Israel.

The climax of their negotiations? Richard proposes that his sister Joanna should marry Saladin's brother Safadin and that they rule an Islamic-Christian kingdom—together in Jerusalem under Saladin's crown. Amazingly, Saladin agrees in principle, calling Richard's bluff: unsurprisingly, his sister Joanna refuses to marry a Muslim, even a king of Jerusalem. There is something very modern in their letters—in today's peace process, this time between Israel and the Palestinians, Jerusalem remains the thorniest issue. Unsurprisingly, the plan fails—as have many other plans to make peace in the Middle East.

Richard to Saladin

Men of ours and of yours have died, the country is in ruins, and events have entirely escaped anyone's control. Do you not believe that it is enough? As far as we are concerned, there are only three subjects of

discord: Jerusalem, the True Cross, and territory. As for
Jerusalem, it is our place of worship and we will never
agree to renounce it, even if we have to fight to the last
man. As territory, all we want is that the land west of
the Jordan be ceded to us. As for the Cross, for you it
is merely a piece of wood, whereas for us its value is
inestimable. Let the Sultan give it to us, and let us put
an end to this exhausting struggle.

Saladin to Richard

Jerusalem is holy to us as well as to you, and more so,
seeing it is the scene of our Prophet's journey, and the
place where our people must assemble at the Last Day.
Think not that we shall go back therefrom, or that we
can be compliant in this matter. And as for the land,
it was ours to begin with, and you invaded it: nor
[would you have taken it] but for the feebleness of the
Muslims who then had it; and so long as this war lasts
God will not permit you to set up a stone in it. And
as for the Cross, our holding it is a point of vantage,
nor can we surrender it except for some benefit of
Islam.

Arthur James Balfour to Lord Rothschild, 2 November 1917

The letter that changed the Middle East. Ever since the Jewish Temple was destroyed by Titus Caesar in AD 70, Jews had
revered Zion and dreamed of a return to Jerusalem. In the late
nineteenth century vicious persecutions in Russia—home to

six million Jews—and anti-Semitic attacks spanning France to Austria, inspired a modern Zionist movement. Even before the First World War, many leading British statesmen were sympathetic to the history and the plight of the Jews, but the circumstances of the war made it possible. In 1917 British troops were poised to invade Palestine, which had been ruled by the Ottoman sultans for four centuries, but the British were also desperate, after years of bloody stalemate on the western front, to keep both Russia and the United States in the war. Both contained large Jewish populations.

Foreign Secretary Balfour writes a letter—"the Balfour Declaration"—which promises the creation of a Jewish national home in the Holy Land without prejudicing the rights of the Arab population already living there. It takes the form of a public letter to one of the leaders of the Jewish community, Walter Rothschild, 2nd Baron, head of the Zionist Federation. In 1948, the state of Israel was created.

Dear Lord Rothschild,

I have much pleasure in conveying to you, on behalf of His Majesty's Government, the following declaration of sympathy with Jewish Zionist aspirations which has been submitted to, and approved by, the Cabinet:

> *His Majesty's Government view with favor the establishment in Palestine of a national home for the Jewish people, and will use their best endeavors to facilitate the achievement of this object, it being clearly understood that nothing shall be done which may prejudice the civil and religious rights of existing non-Jewish communities in Palestine, or the rights*

and political status enjoyed by Jews in any other country.

I should be grateful if you would bring this declaration to the knowledge of the Zionist Federation.

Yours,
Arthur James Balfour

George H. W. Bush to Bill Clinton, 20 January 1993

Here's a letter that defines big-hearted statesmanship in our mean-spirited era. George H. W. Bush was one of the best-qualified US presidents of modern times and the very definition of an American upper-class gentleman. A war-hero pilot who had been shot down in the Second World War, he made a fortune in oil, then was elected to the House of Representatives before serving as ambassador to the UN, envoy to China, and director of the CIA. He then became Ronald Reagan's vice president and succeeded him as the forty-first president. Neither a brilliant statesman nor a charismatic visionary, he was a somewhat uninspiring if steady servant of the nation. He was bemused and alarmed by the fall of the Soviet Union and rather late to adapt to the reality of newly independent states like Russia and Ukraine. But he reacted to the Iraqi dictator Saddam Hussein's invasion of Kuwait by putting together a coalition that liberated the country and hobbled the tyrant while leaving him in power. Faced with the brash energy of the young governor of Arkansas, Bill Clinton, he looked old-fashioned and out of touch in a bruising campaign.

Yet, upon losing his beloved presidency, he sits and writes this charming and magnanimous letter, which he leaves on his desk in the Oval Office for his rival, Clinton. From the last of the old-fashioned war-generation leaders, here is a master class in dutiful service, personal decency, and respect for your opponents. This is how power should change hands in a liberal democracy.

Dear Bill,

When I walked into this office just now I felt the same sense of wonder and respect that I felt four years ago. I know you will feel that, too.

I wish you great happiness here. I never felt the loneliness some Presidents have described.

There will be very tough times, made even more difficult by criticism you may not think is fair. I'm not a very good one to give advice; but just don't let the critics discourage you or push you off course.

You will be <u>our</u> President when you read this note. I wish you well. I wish your family well.

Your success is now our country's success. I am rooting hard for you.

Good luck—
George

Niccolò Machiavelli to Francesco Vettori, 3 August 1514

The Italian politician Niccolò Machiavelli was also a wry observer of human nature. He was at the peak of his professional powers between 1498 and 1512, when he served as secretary to the Second Chancery of the Republic of Florence. Losing favor after a coup the following year, he was arrested and tortured, finally being released to his estate where he relaxed, walked, read

poetry, and wrote his most famous work, *The Prince*, which, using
the rise and fall of his contemporary Cesare Borgia, analyzed
the conduct of politicians with amoral realism: "Whether it be
better to be loved than feared or feared than loved? One should
wish to be both not because it is difficult to unite them in one
person, it is much safer to be feared than loved." His letters,
often to his friend Francesco Vettori, Florentine ambassador in
Rome, are not always political. In this one, dated 5 January 1514,
he recommends the pleasures of love in all its varieties, straight
or gay—a charming definition of rather unMachiavellian tolerance: "He who is deemed wise during the day will never be
considered crazy at night, and he who is esteemed a respectable
man, and is worthy, whatever he does to lighten his heart and
live happily renders him honour, not blame. Rather being called
a bugger or a whoremonger, one says he is a man of broad interests, easygoing, and a good fellow."

In this letter, written a few months later, he writes beautifully about falling in love at the age of fifty:

> My friend . . . I have encountered a creature so gracious,
> so delicate . . . that I cannot praise her so much or
> love her so much that she would not deserve more. I
> ought to tell you with what nets of gold, spread among
> flowers, woven by Venus, so pleasant and easy that a
> villainous heart might have broken. . . . You should not
> believe that Love in order to take me has used ordinary
> methods, because knowing they would not have been
> enough for him, he used extraordinary ones of which
> I knew nothing and from which I could not protect
> myself. May it be enough for you that already near fifty
> years neither do these suns harm me, nor do rough,
> roads tire me, nor dark hours of night frighten me.
> Everything seems to me level and all her desires. . . .

I adapt myself. . . . I feel in it such sweetness both
through what that face so soft and wonderful brings
me, and also through having laid aside the memory
of all my troubles, that for anything in the world,
being able to free myself I would not wish it. I have
abandoned then the thoughts of affairs great and
serious . . . they are all turned into soft conversations
for which I thank Venus. So if it occurs to you to write
anything about the lady write it. . . . Farewell.

Henry VII to his "good friends," July 1485

It looks like a crazy adventure. On 7 August 1485, Henry Tudor
and a small army of two thousand French mercenaries land
in Wales, determined to seize the kingdom of England from
King Richard III. Henry's claim to the throne is through his
mother, Lady Margaret Beaufort, the great-granddaughter of
John of Gaunt, fourth son of Edward III; he is also descended
from a minor Welsh soldier, Owen Tudor, who had married
Henry V's widow. However tenuous this connection may be,
many better claimants are dead, and everyone knows that Richard III has usurped the throne from his own nephews: the
two young princes have vanished, in the summer of 1483, murdered on Richard's orders. The taint of regicide and infanticide
is pungent.

A year earlier, Henry Tudor had attempted an invasion that
had failed. Now he issues this open letter to potential followers
among the noble magnates. The timing is perfect—rarely has a
political letter been so successful. As he marches into England,
more and more grandees support him.

At the Battle of Bosworth Field on 22 August, various key
magnates, above all the Stanleys, switch sides. Richard loses the

battle, killed in the field. The penniless half-Welsh claimant, who lacks even the proper clothes to wear at his own court, has founded the Tudor dynasty.

> Right trusty, worshipful and honorable good friends,
> and our allies, I greet you well. Being given to
> understand your good devoir and intent to advance me
> to the furtherance of my rightful claim due and lineal
> inheritance of the crown, and for the just depriving of
> that homicide and unnatural tyrant which now unjustly
> bears dominion over you, I give you to understand
> that no Christian heart can be more full of joy upon
> the instance of your sure advertise what powers ye
> will make ready and what captains and leaders you
> get to conduct, be prepared to pass over the sea with
> such forces as my friends are preparing for me. And
> if you have such good speed and success as I wish,
> according to your desire, I shall be ever most forward
> to remember and wholly to requite this your great and
> most loving kindness in my just quarrel.

Given under our signet,
HR

John Adams to Thomas Jefferson,
20 February 1801

The handover of power is a test of every system—but even when it runs smoothly it is often extremely awkward. John Adams was the second US president, whose administration had been something of a mess. He was also the first president to live in the White House. His vice president had been his old comrade Thomas Jefferson, with whom he enjoyed a close and long but touchy relationship. After the 1800 election, when Adams sees his party wiped out, he unworthily tries to stack governmental appointments against the incoming President Jefferson, who denounces this perfidy. Hence Adams's letter is frostily concerned not with the handover of the sacred altar of democracy but with the correct number of horses. After a long sulk on Adams's part and two successful terms of the Jeffersonian presidency, they became friends again in 1811.

Sir

In order to save you the trouble and Expence of purchasing Horses and Carriages, which will not be necessary, I have to inform you that I shall leave in the stables of the United States seven Horses and two Carriages with Harness the Property of the United States. These may not be suitable for you: but they will certainly save you a considerable Expence as they belong to the stud of the President's Household.

I have the Honor to be with great respect, Sir, your most obedient and humble Servant.

Between the Duke of Marlborough, Queen Anne, and Sarah, Duchess of Marlborough,
13 August 1704

A triangle of power, victory, and love, all recorded in intimate letters. Anne, daughter of James II, was the needy, awkward Protestant queen, an unlikely monarch to oversee the defeat of Louis XIV's attempt to dominate Europe. Anne was tormented by ill health and obesity, a condition exacerbated by the misery of seventeen unsuccessful pregnancies with her husband, Prince Georg of Denmark.

The second of this trio was the general John Churchill. On the succession of James II in 1685, he initially backed the king but he sympathized with Protestant Whiggery instead of James's Catholic absolutism. In 1688, when William of Orange (who was married to Mary, another of James II's daughters), landed in England, Churchill supported the Glorious Revolution— and was rewarded with the earldom of Marlborough.

Meeting the strong-willed Sarah Jennings, aged fifteen, at court, Marlborough fell in love and married her just as Sarah became best friends with Anne, now heir to the throne. Anne looked to Sarah for emotional sustenance, writing her such passionate letters that Sarah later accused her of lesbianism. "I hope I shall get a moment or two to be with my dear," writes Anne to Sarah. "That I may have one dear embrace which I long for more than I can express." To ensure secrecy in their letter writing, they called each other Mrs. Morley and Mrs. Freeman.

In 1702, when Anne succeeds to the throne, Britain is fighting France, and Marlborough, now captain-general, wins an unbroken series of victories. Here, after Blenheim, his greatest victory, he writes to Sarah to tell the queen instead of writing to Anne directly, consolidating Sarah's importance. Marlborough received a dukedom and Blenheim Palace, but ultimately, Mrs. Morley and Mrs. Freeman fell out viciously, contributing to Marlborough's fall and the end of the war.

> I have not time to say more, but beg you will give
> my duty to the Queen and let her know her army
> has had a glorious victory. M Tallard [Marshal of

France] and two other generals are in my coach and I am following the rest. The bearer, my aide de camp Colonel Parke, will give her an account of what has passed. I shall do it in a day or two by another more at large.

Donald J. Trump to Kim Jong Un, 24 May 2018

A letter characteristic of the world-changing style of President Donald Trump. Considering himself to be a global dealmaker, if only trained by his experiences in global real estate and US reality television, Trump believes that his personal diplomacy at summit meetings can achieve deals unreachable by more conventional politicians.

In early 2018, he is convinced that if he is able to meet with the youthful North Korean dictator Kim Jong Un, he can solve the dangerous problem of the nuclear arsenal built by the Kim dynasty to protect their seventy-year rule. When North Korean negotiators turn hostile, Trump turns to the old-fashioned diplomatic letter, a form that may appeal to the rigid Stalinist formality of the dynasty. But its tone is typical of this presidency. Highly Trumpian in its bombastic swagger, theatrical menace, and plangent sentimentality, it is perhaps the first letter in which a US president so brazenly trumpets his nuclear power and threatens to unleash its apocalyptic force. The letter works. Kim replies with his own formal letter of reconciliation.

The spectacular summit was held in Singapore on 12 June, but the real denuclearization of Korea would be harder to achieve. Nonetheless, this exchange of letters is typical of a strange time in world affairs.

THE WHITE HOUSE
WASHINGTON DC
MAY 24 2018

HIS EXCELLENCY KIM JONG UN
CHAIRMAN OF THE STATE AFFAIRS COMMISSION
OF THE DEMOCRATIC PEOPLE'S REPUBLIC OF KOREA

Dear Mr. Chairman:

We greatly appreciate your time, patience, and effort
with respect to our recent negotiations and discussions
relative to a summit long sought by both parties. . . .
I was very much looking forward to being there with
you. Sadly, based on the tremendous anger and open
hostility displayed in your most recent statement, I
feel it is inappropriate, at this time, to have this long-
planned meeting. . . . You talk about your nuclear
capabilities, but ours are so massive and powerful that
I pray to God they will never have to be used. . . . If
you change your mind having to do with this most
important summit, please do not hesitate to call me
or write. The world, and North Korea in particular,
has lost a great opportunity for lasting peace and great
prosperity and wealth. This missed opportunity is a
truly sad moment in history.

Sincerely yours, Donald J Trump.
President of the United States of America

Downfall

Abd al-Rahman III to his sons, AD 961

Abd al-Rahman was the most magnificent of the Arab rulers of al-Andalus, the Muslim kingdom of Spain. He was descended from Abd al-Rahman I, the Ummayad prince who had escaped from Baghdad (ruled by his enemies the Abbasid caliphs) traveled in disguise across Africa, and then founded his own realm in Spain. After his death the kingdom had declined until the succession of Abd al-Rahman III in 912. A superb general and merciless politician, he embarked on decades of war to defeat all rivals, Muslim and Christian, and dominate Iberia to such an extent that in 929, he declared himself Caliph—Commander of the Faithful—in a letter to the world that damned the Abbasid caliphs of Baghdad as fakes: "We are the most worthy to fulfil our right, and the most entitled to complete our good fortune, and to put on the clothing granted by the nobility of God, because of the favor which He has shown us, and the renown which He has given us, and the power to which He has raised us. . . . We have decided that the acclamation should be to us as Commander of the Faithful. . . . Everyone who calls himself by this name apart from ourselves is arrogating it to himself and trespassing upon it. . . ."

As the seventy-year-old caliph lies dying in 961, the most glorious monarch of his time, he writes this letter, supposedly left for his successor, which is the very definition of humility from the most powerful of rulers: in fifty years of victory, just fourteen days of pleasure.

> I have now reigned above fifty years in victory or peace, beloved by my subjects, dreaded by my enemies, and respected by my allies. Riches and honors, power and pleasure, have waited on my call, nor does any earthly blessing appear to have been wanting to my felicity. In this situation, I have diligently numbered the days of pure and genuine happiness which have fallen to my lot: they amount to FOURTEEN:—O man! place not thy confidence in this present world!

Simon Bar Kokhba to Yeshua, c.AD 135

In 130, Roman Emperor Hadrian visited Jerusalem, in ruins since the destruction of the Temple and city by Titus in 70, and decided to refound it as a pagan city, named after himself and featuring a temple of Jupiter on the site of the Holy of Holies. In 132, a mysterious leader calling himself the Prince of Israel led a powerful rebellion that swiftly destroyed two Roman legions. This was the start of a new Jewish revolt under the command of the prince whose name was probably Shimon ben Kosiba, though his followers hailed him as Simon Bar Kokhba, Son of the Star.

Hadrian rushed reinforcements to crush this new state of Israel but it took three tough years of fighting: finally in 135, Simon was besieged and killed in his fortress of Betar; Hadrian's revenge on the Jews was almost genocidal—the sources claim 500,000 were slaughtered; Jerusalem was renamed Aelia Capitolina after Hadrian's family and became a pagan city; Judea was renamed Palestina. Amazingly in 1960, fifteen of Simon's letters were found in a Judean cave and here is one. Archeologists debate the meaning of the word "destroy," which is damaged and hard to decipher: it was thought at one point that S.B.K. was telling Yeshua to protect the Galileans but now it seems he was telling him to do something bad to them. This correspondence probably dates from the last days of the revolt as the prince struggles to keep control over his diminishing forces. The downfall of the last Jewish state (until 1948) is close.

> From Shimon ben Kosiba to Yeshua ben Galgoula
> and the men of the fortress. Peace to you. Heaven is
> my witness against me that unless you destroy the
> Galileans who are with you down to the last man, I
> shall, as I did to ben Aphul, put fetters on your feet.

Ammurapi to the king of Alashiya, c.1190 BC

Around 1190 BC, an army of seafaring marauders attacked a prosperous Syrian city, Ugarit, which had close relations with other powers of the late Bronze Age world: Egypt to the south and the Hittites to the north. As the marauders attack, the king of Ugarit, Ammurapi, appeals to his Alashiyan (Cypriot) neighbor. We still do not know the identity of the aggressors, so they are known as the Sea Peoples. In this letter, Ammurapi recounts the beginning of the destruction of his kingdom. Even reading it three thousand years later, its desperation is tangible—and no wonder. The Sea Peoples destroyed many of the empires of the day.

> My father, behold, the enemy's ships came [here];
> my cities were burned, and they did evil things in my
> country. Does not my father know that all my troops

and chariots are in the Land of Hatti, and all my ships
are in the Land of Lukka? . . . Thus, the country is
abandoned to itself. May my father know it: the seven
ships of the enemy that came here inflicted much
damage upon us.

Aurangzeb to his son Muhammad Azam Shah, 1707

A letter of humility before death, from a man of intolerant
power. Aurangzeb "the world-seizer" was the last great Mughal
emperor of India. He was born the third son of Shah Jahan,
builder of the Taj Mahal. After a struggle for power in which he
brutally executed all his rival brothers, he humiliated his father,
then imposed a severe Islamic regime on the multireligious,
multiethnic empire, dangerously weakening it. After crushing
rebellions from Hindus and Sikhs, Aurangzeb lies dying, filled
with regrets and doubts, and writes this to his son.

Health to thee! My heart is near thee. Old age is
arrived: weakness subdues me, and strength has
forsaken all my members. I came a stranger into this
world, and a stranger I depart. I know nothing of
myself, what I am, and for what I am destined. The
instant which passed in power, hath left only sorrow
behind it. I have not been the guardian and protector of
the empire. My valuable time has been passed vainly. I
had a patron in my own dwelling [he probably means
his conscience], but his glorious light was unseen by
my dim sight. Life is not lasting; there is no vestige of
departed breath, and all hopes from futurity are lost.
The fever has left me, but nothing of me remains but
skin and bone. My son [Kaum Buksh], though gone

toward Beejapore, is still near; and thou, my son, art yet nearer. The worthy of esteem, Shaw Aulum, is far distant; and my grandson [Azeem Ooshawn], by the orders of God, is arrived near Hindustan. The camp and followers, helpless and alarmed, are, like myself, full of affliction, restless as the quicksilver. Separated from their lord, they know not if they have a master or not.

I brought nothing into this world, and, except the infirmities of man, carry nothing out. I have a dread for my salvation, and with what torments I may be punished. Though I have strong reliance on the mercies and bounty of God, yet, regarding my actions, fear will not quit me; but, when I am gone, reflection will not remain. Come what may, I have launched my vessel to the waves. Though Providence will protect the camp, yet, regarding appearances, the endeavors of my sons are indispensably incumbent. Give my last prayers to my grandson [Bedar Bakht], whom I cannot see, but the desire affects me. The Begum [his daughter] appears afflicted; but God is the only judge of hearts. The foolish thoughts of women produce nothing but disappointment. Farewell! farewell! farewell!

Simón Bolívar to José Flores, 9 November 1830

All political careers end in failure but this is political despondency. Simón Bolívar has liberated half of South America from Spanish rule and served as president of Gran Colombia, dictator of Peru, and much else, but his career ends catastrophically in the collapse of his authority and the state he has created. He retires on 20 January 1830. After the assassination of his closest ally, Marshal José de Sucre, he is in despair. Already dying, he

writes to President Flores of Ecuador: "Avenge Sucre's murder . . . then get out while you can." Soon after delivering this
damning assessment of South America's future, he died of
tuberculosis, aged just forty-five.

> Use the past to predict the future. You know that I
> have ruled for twenty years, and I have derived from
> these only a few sure conclusions: . . . 1. America is
> ungovernable; 2. He who serves a revolution plows
> the sea; 3. all one can do in America is leave it; 4. the
> country is bound to fall into unimaginable chaos, after
> which it will pass into the hands of an indistinguishable
> string of tyrants of every color and races; 5. once we
> are devoured by all manner of crime and reduced to a
> frenzy of violence, no one—not even the Europeans—
> will want to subjugate us; 6. and, finally, if mankind
> could revert to its primitive state, it would be here in
> America, in her final hour.

Goodbye

Leonard Cohen to Marianne Ihlen, July 2016

Saying goodbye is one of the arts of letter writing. No other singer-songwriter between the 1960s and the start of the twenty-first century was such a master of words, as well as music, as Leonard Cohen. He regarded himself primarily as a poet, but it is the lyrics and songs that are his masterpieces, many of them based on his love affairs with women who became his muses—songs such as "Suzanne" and "Seems So Long Ago, Nancy" and "Sisters of Mercy"—but no one inspired him more than Marianne Ihlen, a young Norwegian who in 1960 moved to live with Cohen on the island of Hydra in Greece. She inspired many of his greatest songs, such as "Bird on the Wire" and, above all, "So Long, Marianne."

After they broke up in the late 1960s, she married and moved to Oslo. Many years later, in 2016, she was diagnosed with leukemia. She was failing fast in the hospital and expected to die soon. On 1 July she asks her close friend Jan Christian Mollestad to notify Leonard Cohen, who, at eighty-two, is still singing and writing, though he, too, is ill. Jan sends a letter that night to Cohen, telling him Marianne has "only a few days to live" and ending, "I hope you read this in time to reach her. And I hope you don't think I am interfering. I just pass on Marianne's deep love for you." Jan does not have much hope that he will receive a reply, but at dawn, after a sleepless night, he finds this beautiful letter. Jan reads it to her. "These seven sentences from Leonard—this sign of everlasting affection—gave Marianne a new level of peace." She falls into a coma a day later, dying two days afterward. Leonard Cohen himself died that November. Maybe he saw Marianne "down the road."

> Dearest Marianne,
>   I'm just a little behind you, close enough to take your hand. This old body has given up, as yours has too, and the eviction notice is on its way any day now.
>   I've never forgotten your love and your beauty. But you know that. I don't have to say more.
>   Safe travels, old friend.
>   See you down the road.
>
> *Endless love*
> *and gratitude,*
> Leonard

"Henriette" to Giacomo Casanova, autumn 1749

This is the classic end-of-the-affair letter. The adventurer Giacomo Casanova is celebrated as a prolific lover, who commented, "I have loved women to a frenzy," but he was also variously a librarian, spy, occultist, sponger, fraudster, and fantasist—as well as a wonderful letter writer and memoirist. His first sexual adventure with a pair of sisters launched him on a career as a womanizer, but he was never as cold hearted as he claimed with his 132 paramours, and he loved intelligent women: "conversation is two-thirds of pleasure," he said.

Casanova receives this letter from the one woman he may

have truly loved: the pseudonymous Henriette, whom he met in early 1749 in Parma. Free-spirited and a brilliant conversationalist with superb taste, "those who believe a woman is incapable of making a man happy twenty-four hours a day have never known a Henriette." She was probably a Provençal noblewoman trapped in an unhappy marriage; but it is she, rather than he, who eventually ends it, leaving him a gift of five hundred louis and scratching with a diamond on the window: "You will forget Henriette too."

Her letter is utterly charming—"Let us swear never to forget one another." One presumes she is returning to her boring husband. As so often in such scenarios, the writer swears never to have another illicit affair, but wishes the heartbroken Casanova many other Henriettes: "you will love again." But he knows it will never be the same—there is only one Henriette in a life.

They did meet again—in 1769, when she was fifty-one. When Casanova initially failed to recognize her, she commented— "Plumpness has altered my physiognomy." Her true identity is still unknown.

It is I, dearest and best friend, who have been
compelled to abandon you, but do not let your grief
be increased by any thought of my sorrow. Let us be
wise enough to suppose that we have had a happy
dream, and not to complain of destiny, for never did
so beautiful a dream last so long! Let us be proud of
the consciousness that for three months we gave one
another the most perfect felicity. Few human beings
can boast of so much! Let us swear never to forget one
another, and to often remember the happy hours of
our love, in order to renew them in our souls, which,

although divided, will enjoy them as acutely as if our hearts were beating one against the other. Do not make any enquiries about me, and if chance should let you know who I am, forget it for ever. I feel certain that you will be glad to hear that I have arranged my affairs so well that I shall, for the remainder of my life, be as happy as I can possibly be without you, dear friend, by my side. I do not know who you are, but I am certain that no one in the world knows you better than I do. I shall not have another lover as long as I live, but I do not wish you to imitate me. On the contrary I hope that you will love again, and I trust that a good fairy will bring along your path another Henriette.

Farewell . . . farewell.

Winston Churchill to his wife, Clementine, 17 July 1915

As the world careened into the First World War in 1914, Winston Churchill, aged forty-one, was serving in the cabinet as First Lord of the Admiralty in the charge of the fleet of the world's paramount sea power. Like everyone else in Europe, he was horrified by the purblind, feverish stagger into war, writing to his wife, Clementine, in July 1914: "I cannot feel that we in this island are in any serious degree responsible for the wave of madness which has swept the mind of Christendom. No one can measure the consequences. I wondered whether those stupid Kings and Emperors could not assemble together and revivify kingship by saving the nations from hell but we all drift on in a kind of dull cataleptic trance." Once the initial German attacks against France and Russia had failed to knock them out of the war, the war descended into a murderous trench warfare, which Churchill tried to solve in an imaginative way by suggesting an attack on the weakest link among Germany's allies, the Ottoman Empire, thereby relieving pressure on the Russians and hopefully capturing Istanbul. This was a sensible idea, but it was appallingly executed, and it became the disastrous Gallipoli campaign. Churchill was removed from the Admiralty and demoted. He resigned in November 1915 to serve in the trenches as a lieutenant-colonel, returning to the government in July 1917.

It is during his political limbo preparing to enlist that he writes this letter to Clementine to be opened "in the event of my death." Mentioning his son Randolph as his heir, Churchill treats Clementine with a characteristic combination of political pragmatism, bumptious self-confidence, romantic love, and a chivalric, even spiritual, open-mindedness, especially his promise that "if there is anywhere else I shall be on the lookout for you."

In the event of my death.

I am anxious that you should get hold of all my papers, especially those which refer to my Admiralty administration. I have appointed you my sole literary executor. . . . There is no hurry; but some day I should like the truth to be known. Randolph will carry on the lamp. Do not grieve for me too much. I am a spirit confident of my rights. Death is only an incident, and not the most important which happens to us in this state of being. On the whole, especially since I met you my darling one, I have been happy, and you have taught me how noble a woman's heart can be. If there is anywhere else I shall be on the lookout for you. Meanwhile look forward, feel free, rejoice in life, cherish the children, guard my memory. God bless you. Goodbye. W

Nikolai Bukharin to Josef Stalin, 10 December 1937

A letter of devotion and submission from a man to his killer. This is one of the strangest letters in this book, both heartbreaking and horrific, reflecting the bizarre murderous frenzy of the Great Terror in Soviet Russia. In the late 1920s, Josef Stalin and Nikolai Bukharin had been intimate friends and political allies in ruling the Soviet Union. Their wives were friends; their families ran in and out of each other's houses. Bukharin was an intellectual described by Lenin as "the darling of the Party." But in 1929, Stalin turned against Bukharin, who in turn plotted with Stalin's enemies and continued to be friends with Stalin's wife, Nadezhda. Nadezhda Stalin committed suicide in 1932. As for Bukharin, he divorced his own first wife, also named Nadezhda, and married Anna, the teenage daughter of a well-known Party leader. During the thirties, Stalin toyed with Bukharin until 1936, when he launched a purge of the Bolshevik leadership, orchestrating the destruction of his former friend. The Terror intensified as Stalin arranged the arrest, torture, and execution of around a million people. Finally, Bukharin was arrested and forced to confess to crimes he did not commit.

Knowing he is likely to be shot by the remorseless Stalin, he writes a final letter from prison. Yet, as a Bolshevik devoted to the Marxist-Leninist mission before everything, even his own life, he expresses devotion to Stalin—his friend, "Koba"—and to the Communist Party and admires the big idea of a brutal purge. Bukharin is clearly exhausted, desperate, almost feverish, and rambling as he dreams of meeting his own wife, Nadezhda, again; begs to see his young wife one last time; fears the bullets; and requests morphine. The letter is extraordinary in its mixture of love and humiliation—and in Bukharin's readiness to die for the Party, confessing crimes he never committed.

Stalin wanted Bukharin to die, and he was executed after his public trial on 15 March 1938. Stalin is said to have kept this letter in his desk for the rest of his life.

VERY SECRET

PERSONAL

REQUEST NO ONE BE ALLOWED TO *READ* THIS LETTER WITHOUT THE EXPRESS PERMISSION OF I.V. STALIN.

Josef Vissarionovich:

This is perhaps the last letter I shall write to you before my death. That's why, though I am a prisoner, I ask you to permit me to write this letter without resorting to officialese, all the more so since I am writing this letter to you alone: the very fact of its existence or nonexistence will remain entirely in your hands.

I've come to the last page of my drama and perhaps of my very life. I agonized over whether I should pick up pen and paper—as I write this, I am shuddering all over from disquiet and from a thousand emotions stirring within me, and I can hardly control myself. But precisely because I have so little time left, I want to *take my leave* of you in advance, before it's too late, before my hand ceases to write, before my eyes close, while my brain somehow still functions.

In order to avoid any misunderstandings, I will say to you from the outset that, as far as *the world at large* (society) is concerned: a) I have no intention of recanting anything I've written down [confessed]; b) In *this* sense (or in connection with this), I have no intention of asking you or pleading with you for anything that might derail my case from the direction in which it is heading. But I am writing to you for your *personal* information. I cannot leave this life without writing to you these last lines because I am in the grip of torments which you should know about. . . .

There is something *great and bold about the political idea* of a general purge. It is a) connected with the pre-war situation and b) connected with the transition to democracy. This purge encompasses 1) the guilty; 2) persons under suspicion; and 3) persons potentially under suspicion. This business could not have been managed without me. Some are neutralized one way, others in another way, and a third group in yet another way. What serves as a guarantee for all is the fact that people inescapably talk about each other and in doing so arouse an *everlasting* distrust in each other. . . . In this way, the leadership is bringing about a *full guarantee* for itself.

For God's sake, don't think that I am engaging here in reproaches, even in my inner thoughts. I wasn't born yesterday. I know all too well that *great* plans, *great* ideas, and *great* interests take precedence over everything, and I know that it would be petty for me to place the question of my own person *on a par* with the *universal-historical* tasks resting, first and foremost on your shoulders. . . .

Permit me, finally, to move on to my last, minor, requests.

a) It would be a thousand times easier for me *to die* than to go through the coming trial: I simply don't know how I'll be able to control myself—you know my nature: I am not an enemy either of the party or of the USSR, and I'll do all within my

powers [to serve my party's cause], but, under such
circumstances, my powers are minimal, and heavy
emotions rise up in my soul. . . .

b) If I'm to receive the death sentence, then I implore
you beforehand, I entreat you, by all that you hold
dear, not to have me shot. Let me drink poison in
my cell instead. (Let me have morphine so that I can
fall asleep and never wake up.) For me, this point
is extremely important. I don't know what words I
should summon up in order to entreat you to grant
me this as an act of charity. After all, politically, it
won't really matter, and, besides, no one will know a
thing about it. But let me spend my last moments as
I wish. Have pity on me! Surely you'll understand—
knowing me as well as you do. Sometimes I look
death openly in the face, just as I know very well that
I am capable of brave deeds. At other times, I, ever
the same person, find myself in such disarray that I
am drained of all strength. So if the verdict is death,
let me have a cup of morphine. I *implore* you. . . .

c) I ask you to allow me to bid farewell to my wife and
son. No need for me to say goodbye to my daughter. I
feel sorry for her. It will be too painful for her. It
will also be too painful for Nadya [Bukharin's first
wife] and my father. Anyuta, on the other hand, is
young. She will survive. I would like to exchange
a few last words with her. I would like permission to
meet her *before* the trial. My argument is as follows: if
my family sees what I *confessed* to, they might commit
suicide from sheer unexpectedness. I must somehow
prepare them for it. It seems to me that this is in the
interests of the case and its official interpretation.

d) If, contrary to expectation, my life is to be spared,

I would like to request (though I would first have to discuss it with my wife) . . . That I be exiled to America for x number of years. . . . But if there is the slightest doubt in your mind, then exile me to a camp in *Pechora* or *Kolyma,* even for 25 years. . . .

Josef Vissarionovich! In me you have lost one of your most capable generals, one who is genuinely devoted to you. But that is all past. . . . I am preparing myself mentally to depart from this vale of tears, and there is nothing in me toward all of you, toward the party and the cause, but a great and boundless love. I am doing everything that is humanly possible and impossible. I have written to you about all this. I have crossed all the t's and dotted all the i's. I have done all this *in advance,* since I have no idea at all what condition I shall be in tomorrow and the day after tomorrow, etc. Being a neurasthenic, I shall perhaps feel such universal apathy that I won't be able to even so much as move my finger.

But now, in spite of a headache and with tears in my eyes, I am writing. My conscience is clear before you now, Koba. I ask you one final time for your forgiveness (only in your heart, not otherwise). For that reason I embrace you in my mind. Farewell forever and remember kindly your wretched

N. Bukharin

Franz Kafka to Max Brod, June 1924

Franz Kafka wrote of alienation, secrecy, and persecution by sinister bureaucracies, and his last letter to his best friend, Max Brod, displayed all the themes of his works. Born in Prague, Kafka was a Jewish insurance official turned novelist who produced masterpieces such as *The Trial* and *The Castle* and was an obsessional womanizer, yet simultaneously he was tormented by the fear of literary and sexual failure. He therefore destroyed 90 percent of what he wrote. While he is dying of tuberculosis, he tells Brod to destroy all of his works, which he believed would ruin his literary reputation. Brod chose to ignore his friend's request and between 1925 and 1933 published the work that spawned the term "Kafkaesque."

Dear Max,

My last request: Everything I leave behind me . . . in the way of notebooks, manuscripts, letters, my own and other people's, sketches and so on, is to be burned unread and to the last page, as well as all writings of mine or notes which either you may have or other people, from whom you are to beg them in my name. Letters which are not handed over to you should at least be faithfully burned by those who have them.

Yours,
Franz Kafka

Walter Raleigh to his wife, Bess,
8 December 1603

There is a certain sort of letter by a person who, facing death in the morning, nonetheless manages to write in a fearlessly jaunty tone, and this is one of the best. On 17 November 1603, Sir Walter Raleigh was sentenced to death for treason, thanks to his involvement in the "Main Plot" against the new king James I. The night before his execution he writes this letter to Bess, which contains matter-of-fact financial details, expressions of love for his wife and son, and reflections on death with sentiments of swashbuckling courage and unbearable sadness.

A paragon of his age, Raleigh was a favorite of Elizabeth I—dashingly handsome, an adventurer, privateer, and admiral who founded the first colony in North America, raided Spanish possessions in Latin America, and co-commanded attacks on Spain itself. He was not just a man of action but of letters, too, an acclaimed poet and historian, and a chemist. The morning after this letter was written, Raleigh was taken out to be beheaded, then reprieved by the king at the last moment, but kept in the Tower of London for over a decade—until 1616—giving him the chance to write a history of the world and many other works. He persuaded the king to release him to go off in search of El Dorado (a legendary city of gold that he believed awaited discovery in today's Venezuela). His expedition discovered no gold, which infuriated the king's Spanish allies. The Spanish ambassador demanded Raleigh's head. He was finally executed in 1618. Bess was said to have had Walter's head embalmed and to have carried it around with her until her own death in 1647.

WINCHESTER, 8 DECEMBER 1603

You shall now receive (my dear wife) my last words in these my last lines. My love I send you, that you may keep it when I am dead, and my counsel that you may remember it when I am no more. I would not by my will present you with sorrows (dear Bess). Let them go to the grave with me and be buried in the dust. And seeing that it is not the will of God that I should see you any more in this life, bear it patiently, and with a heart like thy self.

First, I send you all the thanks which my heart can conceive, or my words can express for your many travails, and care taken for me, which, though they have not taken effect as you wished, yet my debt to you is not the less: but pay it I never shall in this world.

Secondly, I beseech you for the love you bear me living, do not hide your self many days, but by your travails seek to help your miserable fortunes and the right of your poor child. Thy mourning cannot avail me, I am but dust.

Thirdly, you shall understand, that my land was conveyed bona fide to my child: the writings were drawn at midsummer twelve months. My honest cousin Brett can testify so much, and Dalberry, too, can remember somewhat therein. And I trust that my blood will quench their malice that have thus cruelly murthered me: and that they will not seek also to kill thee and thine with extreme poverty. To what friend to direct thee I know not, for all mine have left me in the true time of trial. And I plainly perceive that my death was determined from the first day.

Most sorry I am, God knows, that being thus
surprised with death I can leave you in no better estate.
God is my witness I meant you all my office of wines or
all that I could have purchased by selling it, half of my
stuff, and all my jewels, but some of it for the boy. But
God hath prevented all my resolutions, and even great
God that ruleth all in all. But if you live free from want,
care for no more, for the rest is but vanity.

Love God, and begin betimes to repose your self
upon him, and therein shall you find true and lasting
riches, and endless comfort: for the rest when you have
travailed and wearied your thoughts over all sorts of
worldly cogitations, you shall but sit down by sorrow
in the end. Teach your son also to love and fear God
whilst he is yet young, that the fear of God may grow
with him, and the same God will be a husband to you,
and a father to him; a husband and a father which
cannot be taken from you.

Baylie oweth me 200 pounds, and Adrian Gilbert
600. In Jersey I also have much owing me besides.
The arrearages of the wines will pay my debts. And
howsoever you do, for my soul's sake, pay all poor men.
When I am gone, no doubt you shall be sought for by
many, for the world thinks that I was very rich. But
take heed of the pretenses of men, and their affections,
for they last not, but in honest and worthy men, and no
greater misery can befall you in this life, than to become
a prey, and afterward to be despised. I speak not this
(God knows) to dissuade you from marriage, for it
will be best for you, both in respect of the world and
of God.

As for me, I am no more yours, nor you mine. Death
hath cut us asunder and God hath divided me from the

world, and you from me. Remember your poor child for his father's sake, who chose you, and loved you in his happiest times.

Get those letters (if it be possible) which I writ to the Lords, wherein I sued for my life. God is my witness, it was for you and yours that I desired life. But it is true that I disdained my self for begging of it. For know it (my dear wife) that your son is the son of a true man, and one who in his own respect despiseth death and all his misshapen and ugly formes.

I cannot write much. God he knows how hardly I steal this time while others sleep, and it is also time that I should separate my thoughts from the world. Beg my dead body which living was denied thee; and either lay it at Sherburne (and if the land continue) or in Exeter-Church, by my father and mother. I can say no more, time and death call me away.

The everlasting God, powerful, infinite, and omnipotent God, that almighty God, who is goodness it self, the true life and true light keep thee and thine. Have mercy on me, and teach me to forgive my persecutors and false accusers, and send us to meet in his glorious kingdom.

My dear wife farewell. Bless my poor boy. Pray for me, and let my good God hold you both in his arms. Written with the dying hand of sometimes thy husband, but now alas overthrown.

Yours that was, but now not my own.
                                        WR

Alan Turing to Norman Routledge, February 1952

A heartbreaking letter from the time when homosexuality was illegal in the UK. Alan Turing was the computer scientist, mathematician, and cryptographer who had played a crucial role in breaking the Nazi Enigma code during the war, at Bletchley Park, and in developing the Turing test to measure artificial intelligence.

In 1952, Turing was living in Manchester, where he began a relationship with a young man, Arnold Murray. When Murray was burgled, Turing inadvertently revealed his homosexuality during the police investigation, resulting in prosecution for both men for "gross indecency" under the Criminal Law Amendment Act 1885, then used to prosecute homosexuals. Turing pleaded guilty, facing no time in prison provided he underwent a hormonal treatment similar to chemical castration that helped destroy him. This letter to his friend, the mathematician Norman Routledge, indicates the level of anxiety and misery that he is suffering. He committed suicide by biting into a cyanide-poisoned apple on 8 June 1954.

Homosexuality was decriminalized in the UK in 1967, but it was only in 2017 that the "Turing law" formally pardoned Turing and other homosexuals persecuted under the old laws.

My dear Norman,

   I've now got myself into the kind of trouble that I have always considered to be quite a possibility for me, though I have usually rated it at about 10:1 against. I shall shortly be pleading guilty to a charge of sexual offenses with a young man. The story of how it all came to be found out is a long and fascinating one, which I shall have to make into a short story one day, but haven't the time to tell you now. No doubt I shall emerge from it all a different man, but quite who I've not found out.

Glad you enjoyed broadcast. Jefferson certainly was rather disappointing though. I'm afraid that the following syllogism may be used by some in the future.

Turing believes machines think
Turing lies with men
Therefore machines do not think

Yours in distress, Alan

Che Guevara to Fidel Castro, 1 April 1965

The two heroes of the Cuban Revolution. Guevara was a handsome Argentine doctor who, after a motorcycle trip throughout Latin America, joined up with Fidel and Raúl Castro, to lead the Cuban Revolution. In the battle to overthrow dictator Fulgencio Batista, Guevara served as a commander of reckless courage and outstanding organizational skills alongside the Castro brothers. They took the capital in 1959. In power, Che oversaw the firing squads that killed "war criminals," trained the army, and ran the agricultural economy, dominated by sugarcane, as well as steering Cuba into an alliance with the Communist Soviet Union.

Guevara was instrumental in inviting the Soviets to place missiles on the island directed at America, which demanded their removal. Faced with nuclear war with America in the Cuban Missile Crisis, the Soviets withdrew them. Guevara and Castro had been willing to risk nuclear apocalypse. Disillusioned with the Soviet betrayal and perhaps with Castro's dominance, Che seeks new adventure, new revolutions to serve, and writes this letter of goodbye.

Guevara then vanishes—first to fight in Congo and then, leaving a letter to his children—"grow up as good revolutionaries"—to Bolivia. There, aged thirty-nine, he is captured and summarily executed by a CIA-advised rightist militia.

Fidel:

At this moment I remember many things: when I met you in Maria Antonia's house, when you proposed I come along, all the tensions involved in the preparations. One day they came by and asked who should be notified in case of death, and the real possibility of it struck us all. Later we knew it was true, that in a revolution one wins or dies (if it is a real one). Many comrades fell along the way to victory.

Today everything has a less dramatic tone, because we are more mature, but the event repeats itself. I feel that I have fulfilled the part of my duty that tied me to the Cuban revolution in its territory, and I say farewell to you, to the comrades, to your people, who now are mine.

I formally resign my positions in the leadership of the party, my post as minister, my rank of commander, and my Cuban citizenship. Nothing legal binds me to Cuba. The only ties are of another nature—those that cannot be broken as can appointments to posts.

Reviewing my past life, I believe I have worked with sufficient integrity and dedication to consolidate the revolutionary triumph. My only serious failing was not having had more confidence in you from the first moments in the Sierra Maestra, and not having understood quickly enough your qualities as a leader and a revolutionary.

I have lived magnificent days, and at your side I felt the pride of belonging to our people in the brilliant yet sad days of the Caribbean [Cuban Missile] crisis. Seldom has a statesman been more brilliant as you were in those days. I am also proud of having followed you without hesitation, of having identified with your way of thinking and of seeing and appraising dangers and principles.

Other nations of the world summon my modest efforts of assistance. I can do that which is denied you due to your responsibility as the head of Cuba, and the time has come for us to part.

You should know that I do so with a mixture of joy and sorrow. I leave here the purest of my hopes as a builder and the dearest of those I hold dear. And I leave a people who received me as a son. That wounds a part of my spirit. I carry to new battlefronts the faith that you taught me, the revolutionary spirit of my people, the feeling of fulfilling the most sacred of duties: to fight against imperialism wherever it may be. This is a source of strength, and more than heals the deepest of wounds.

I state once more that I free Cuba from all responsibility, except that which stems from its example. If my final hour finds me under other skies, my last thought will be of this people and especially of you. I am grateful for your teaching and your example, to which I shall try to be faithful up to the final consequences of my acts. . . .

I am not sorry that I leave nothing material to

my wife and children; I am happy it is that way. I ask nothing for them, as the state will provide them with enough to live on and receive an education.

I would have many things to say to you and to our people, but I feel they are unnecessary. Words cannot express what I would like them to, and there is no point in scribbling pages.

Robert Ross to More Adey, 14 December 1900

By the time Oscar Wilde was released from hard prison labor for homosexuality, his career had been destroyed and his health wrecked. Traveling on the continent at the turn of the twentieth century, he was working on his poem *The Ballad of Reading Gaol*—"Yet each man kills the thing he loves"— about the hanging of a murderer. He also handed Robbie Ross, his executor, *De Profundis*, a public letter of reproach addressed to his lover and nemesis, Lord Alfred "Bosie" Douglas. After a short reunion with Bosie, Wilde returned to Paris, living at the dire Hôtel d'Alsace in Saint-Germain—"My wallpaper and I are fighting a duel to the death," he remarked. "One of us has got to go." Here his suppurating ear, which had troubled him for a while, became fatal meningitis.

Robbie Ross had always been his most devoted friend: when Wilde came out of jail, Ross alone in a sullen crowd had taken off his hat: "Men have gone to heaven for smaller things than that," Wilde wrote in *De Profundis*. Now Ross and another loyal friend, Reggie Turner, are present at this, Wilde's last scene.

During my absence Reggie went every day to see Oscar, and wrote me short bulletins. Oscar went out several times with him driving, and seemed much better. I had

decided that when I had moved my mother to Menton
on the following Friday, I would go to Paris, but on
the Wednesday evening, at five-thirty, I got a telegram
from Reggie saying "Almost hopeless." I just caught the
express and arrived in Paris at 10:20 in the morning.

   Dr. Tucker informed me that Oscar could not
live for more than two days. His appearance was very
painful. He was trying to speak. He was conscious that
people were in the room, and raised his hand when
I asked him whether he understood. I then went in
search of a priest, and after great difficulty found father
Cuthbert Dunn, of the Passionists, who came with
me at once and administered Baptism and Extreme
Unction—Oscar could not take the Eucharist. You
know I have always promised to bring a priest and I
feel rather guilty that I had so often dissuaded him
from becoming a Catholic, but you know my reasons
for doing so. . . . Reggie and I slept at the hotel that
night in a room upstairs. We were called twice by the
nurse, who thought Oscar was actually dying. At about
5:30 in the morning a complete change came over him,
the lines of the face altered, and I believe what is called
the death rattle began, but I had never heard anything
like it before; it sounded like the horrible turning of
a crank, and it never ceased until the end. Foam and
blood came from his mouth, and had to be wiped away
by someone standing by him all the time. At 12 o'clock
I went out to get some food, Reggie mounting guard.
He went out at 12:30. From 1 o'clock we did not leave
the room; the painful noise from the throat became
louder and louder. Reggie and myself destroyed letters
to keep ourselves from breaking down. The nurse was
out, and the proprietor of the hotel had come to take

her place; at 1:45 the time of his breathing altered. I
went to the bedside and held his hand, his pulse began
to flutter. He heaved a deep sigh, the only natural one
I had heard since I arrived, the limbs seemed to stretch
involuntarily, the breathing became fainter; he passed
away at 10 minutes to 2 p.m. exactly.

After washing and winding the body, and removing
the appalling debris which has to be burnt, Reggie and
myself and the proprietor started for the Mairie to
make the official declarations.

I'm glad to say dear Oscar looked calm and
dignified, just as he did when he came out of prison.
Around his neck was the blessed rosary which you gave
me, and on the breast, a Franciscan medal given me by
one of the nuns. An unsuccessful photograph of Oscar
was taken by Maurice Gilbert at my request but the
flashlight did not work properly.

I can scarcely speak in moderation of the
magnanimity, humanity and charity of Dupoirier, the
proprietor of the Hôtel d'Alsace. Just before I left Paris
Oscar told me he owed him over 190 Pounds. From the
day Oscar was laid up he never said anything about it.
He was present at Oscar's operation, and attended to
him personally every morning, paying for luxuries and
necessities ordered by the doctor out of his own pocket.

Reggie Turner had the worst time of all in many
ways—he experienced all the horrible uncertainty and
the appalling responsibility of which he did not know
the extent. It will always be a source of satisfaction
to those who were very fond of Oscar, that he had
someone like Reggie near him during his last days
while he was articulate and sensible of kindness and
attention.

Lucrezia Borgia to Leo X, 22 June 1519

A letter from a woman dying in childbirth to her priest. Its writer was born Lucrezia Borgia, daughter of the degenerate Pope Alexander VI (born Rodrigo Borgia) and sister of the merciless Cesare. Elected pope in 1492, Rodrigo immediately began to enjoy the riches and pleasures of the papacy and to promote his family's prosperity with more shamelessness and bloodletting than was customary. His eldest son was murdered—most likely by his second son Cesare, who soon became a duke, killing any and all opponents.

Their sister Lucrezia was beautiful, but regarded by many as a she-devil, tainted by the family's crimes. Her husbands and lovers were variously strangled, poisoned, or found floating in the Tiber; and she was said to have had a child by either her father or her brother, who then forced her to marry the future Duke of Este.

When father and brother died, Lucrezia was finally freed of her poisonous family and lived on as Duchess d'Este for fifteen respectable years. Now, at thirty-nine, she gives birth to a daughter but realizes that a postnatal infection has doomed her. She dies two days after writing this to the pope.

Most Holy Father and Honored Master
    With all respect, I kiss your Holiness's feet and commend myself in all humility to your holy mercy. Having suffered for more than two months, early on the morning of the 14th of the present, as it pleased God, I gave birth to a daughter, and hoped then to find relief from my sufferings, but I did not, and shall be compelled to pay my debt to nature. So great is the favor which our merciful Creator has shown me, that I approach the end of life with pleasure, knowing that, in

a few hours, after receiving for the last time all the holy sacraments of the Church, I shall be released. Having arrived at this moment, I desire as a Christian, although I am a sinner, to ask your Holiness, in your mercy, to give me all possible spiritual consolation and your Holiness's blessing for my soul. Therefore I offer myself to you in all humility and commend my husband and my children, all of whom are your servants, to your Holiness's mercy.

Your Holiness's humble servant,
Lucrezia d'Este

Hadrian to Antoninus Pius—and to his soul, 10 July AD 138

No farewell letter from a dying man to his friends could be more elegant than this one. When he writes this elegy for the departure of his soul, Hadrian is dying at his villa at Baiae.

One of the most gifted men to become emperor of Rome, he was a writer, poet, architect, and a restless traveler—in fact, the most traveled of all Roman princeps. He helped design exquisite architecture such as his villa, as well as the Pantheon and his own mausoleum in Rome, the Castel Sant'Angelo. He was married, but his great love was his male lover Antinous; when he died young, Hadrian had him deified. But Hadrian was also a ruthless ruler, executing senators and relatives suspected of treason or driving them to suicide, while his suppression of the Jewish revolt of Simon Bar Kokhba was savage.

Now dying, he writes to his chosen successor and adopted son, Antoninus Pius: "Emperor Caesar Hadrian Augustus to Antoninus, greeting. Above all I want you to know that I am being released from my life neither before my time or unreasonably or piteously nor unexpectedly nor with faculties impaired even though I shall almost seem to do injury to you who are by my side my father fell ill at the age of forty so I have lived twice again as long as him and reached the same age as my mother. . . ." And he most probably includes in the letter this whimsical goodbye to his own soul, one of the best salutations to death ever written:

ANIMULA, VAGULA, BLANDULA,
HOSPES COMESQUE CORPORIS,
QUAE NUNC ABIBIS IN LOCA
PALLIDULA, RIGIDA, NUDULA,
NEC, UT SOLES, DABIS IOCOS

Little soul, little wanderer, little charmer,
body's guest and companion,
to what places will you set out for now?
To darkling, cold and gloomy ones—
and you won't make your usual jokes.

Acknowledgments

I want to thank my colleagues and friends who have helped with brilliant ideas for this book: Tom Holland, Andrew Roberts, Jonathan Foreman, Kate Jarvis, Dr. Lorenza Smith, F. M. Eloischari, and my very well-read mother, April Sebag-Montefiore. Special thanks to Jan Christian Mollestad for telling me the real story of Leonard Cohen's letter to Marianne and allowing me to quote his words. Thank you to my publishers David Shelley and Holly Harley and to my agents Georgina Capel, Rachel Conway, Irene Baldoni, and my movie and TV agent Simon Shaps. Special thanks to my daughter, Lily, for helping me choose the letters on an exciting voyage through my library. Thanks to Alex Larman for additional research. And as always thanks to my darling wife, Santa, my daughter, Lily, and my son, Sasha.

Copyright
Acknowledgments

Nicolson, 2014; p. 53 Joseph II to his brother Leopold II, 4 October 1777: *Joseph II*, Volume 1, "In the Shadow of Maria Theresa," 1741–1780, Derek Beales, Cambridge University Press, 30 April 1987, p. 374. Reproduced with permission from Cambridge University Press; p. 55 Rameses the Great to Ḥattušili III, 1243 BC: *The Kingdom of the Hittites*, Trevor Bryce, Oxford University Press, 2005, p. 284. Reproduced with permission of Oxford University Press; p. 59 Michelangelo to Giovanni da Pistoia, 1509: *"Michelangelo: To Giovanni Da Pistoia When the Author Was Painting the Vault of the Sistine Chapel (by Michelangelo Buonarroti)"* from Zeppo's First Wife, Gail Mazur. Copyright © 2005 by Gail Mazur. Reproduced with permission from G. Mazur; p. 61 Wolfgang Amadeus Mozart to his cousin Marianne, 13 November 1777: *Mozart's Letters, Mozart's Life*, edited and translated by Robert Spaethling, W. W. Norton & Co., 2000. Reproduced with permission from W. W. Norton & Co. and from Faber & Faber Ltd.; p. 64 Honoré de Balzac to Ewelina Hánska, 19 June 1836: *The Letters of Honore de Balzac to Madame Hanska*, translated by Katherine P. Wormeley, Hardy, Pratt and Company, 1900; p. 66 Pablo Picasso to Marie-Thérèse Walter, 19 July 1939: *Picasso: Creator and Destroyer*, Arianna Stassinopoulos Huffington, Weidenfeld & Nicolson, 1988, p. 247; p. 69 T. S. Eliot to George Orwell, 13 July 1944: T. S. Eliot, on behalf of Faber & Faber. © Estate of T. S. Eliot and reprinted by permission of Faber & Faber Ltd. Courtesy of Orwell Archive, UCL Library Services, Special Collections; p. 75 Sarah Bernhardt to Mrs. Patrick Campbell, 1915: *My Life and Some Letters*, Mrs. Patrick Campbell (Beatrice Stella Cornwallis-West), Dodd, Mead and Company, 1922; p. 76 Fanny Burney to her sister Esther, 22 March 1812: Berg Coll MSS Arblay, © Henry W. and Albert A. Berg Collection of English and American Literature, The New York Public Library, Astor, Lenox and Tilden Foundations; p. 82 David Hughes to

1783: *Selected Letters of Marquis de Sade*, edited by Margaret Crosland, Peter Owen, 1965. Reproduced with permission from Peter Owen Publishers UK; p. 179 Between Empress Alexandra and Nicholas II, 1916: *The Romanovs: 1613–1918*, Simon Sebag Montefiore, Weidenfeld & Nicolson, 2016; p. 185 Maria Theresa to Marie Antoinette, 30 July 1775: *Secrets of Marie Antoinette: A Collection of Letters*, edited by Olivier Bernier, Fromm, 1986, p. 172. Reproduced with permission from Olivier Bernier; p. 187 Mahatma Gandhi to Hitler, 24 December 1940: *Letter to Adolf Hitler*, As at Wardha, December 24, 1940; p. 190 Abraham Lincoln to Ulysses S. Grant, 13 July 1863: *Collected Works of Abraham Lincoln*, edited by Roy P. Basler et al., Abraham Lincoln Association, 1953; p. 193 Jacqueline Kennedy to Nikita Khrushchev, 1 December 1963: *The Death of a President*, November 20–November 25, 1963 William Manchester, 1963, pp. 653–4. John F Kennedy Presidential Library; p. 195 Babur to his son Humayun, 11 January 1529: *An Unpublished Testament of Babur*, N. C. Mehta, The Twentieth Century, 1936, p. 340; p. 196 Émile Zola to Félix Faure, 13 January 1898: *L'Aurore*, Jan. 13, 1898, translated by Chameleon Translations; p. 209 Emmeline Pankhurst to the Women's Social and Political Union, 10 January 1913: National Archives; p. 211 Rosa Parks to Jessica Mitford, 26 February 1956: Rosa Parks Papers: General Correspondence, 2006; Alphabetical file; Mitford, *Jessica "Decca" Treuhaft, letter from Parks, 1956*. Rosa Parks used with permission from The Rosa and Raymond Parks Institute for Self-Development. All rights reserved; p. 213 Nelson Mandela to Winnie Mandela, 2 April 1969: *The Prison Letters of Nelson Mandela*, Liveright Publishing Corp., 2018, in cooperation with the Estate of Nelson Mandela and the Nelson Mandela Foundation in South Africa. Reproduced with permission from The Estate of Nelson Mandela; p. 216 Abram Hannibal to Peter the Great, 5 March 1722: *Hannibal: The Moor of Petersburg*, Hugh Barnes, Profile Books, 2006. Courtesy of

Casanova, autumn 1749: *The Memoirs of Jacques Casanova de Seingalt*, Volume 2 "To Paris and Prison," Giacomo Casanova, Start Publishing LLC, 2013; p. 274 Winston Churchill to his wife, Clementine, 1915: Reproduced with permission of Curtis Brown Group Ltd on behalf of The Estate of Sir Winston S. Churchill © The Estate of Winston S. Churchill; p. 281 Franz Kafka to Max Brod, June 1924: *The Trial*, Franz Kafka, translated by Willa and Edwin Muir, Secker, © 1986. All Kafka material is copyrighted by Schocken Books Inc, New York. Translation and Notes © Schocken Books Inc. 1958, 1977. Reproduced with permission from The Random House Group Ltd.; p. 286 Alan Turing to Norman Routledge, February 1952: Unpublished writings of A. M. Turing © copyright The Provost and Scholars of King's College Cambridge 2018. Reproduced with permission; p. 287 Che Guevara to Fidel Castro, 1 April 1965: *The Bolivian Diary of Ernesto Che Guevara*, Ernesto Che Guevara, translated by Michael J. Taber, Pathfinder, 1994, p. 81. El Diario del Che en Bolivia copyright © 1987, 1988 by Editoria Politica. Copyright © 1994 by Pathfinder Press. Reprinted by permission; p. 295 Hadrian to Antoninus Pius—and to his soul, 10 July AD 138: *Hadrian: The Restless Emperor*, Anthony Richard Birley, Psychology Press, 1997, p. 301. Copyright © 1997 Psychology Press. Reproduced with permission from Taylor & Francis Group.